Seen And
An American Girl

Crystina Bass

Copyright © 2022

All Rights Reserved

Table of Contents

Dedication i
Acknowledgment ii
About the Author iii
Preface iv
Chapter 1: You Know 1
Chapter 2: The Child Of A Cuban Princess And A............
Caballero 8
Chapter 3: The Cuban Princess Flees Cuba 18
Chapter 4: Lost & Found 39
Chapter 5: A Night To Remember 51
Chapter 6: Road Trip 1976 58
Chapter 7: Guatemala 65
Chapter 8: Home? 69
Chapter 9: Clear And Present Danger 75
Chapter 10: Mariel Boatlift 84
Chapter 11: Mr. Mom 105
Chapter 12: The Aranzazu 116
Chapter 13: JFK 126
Chapter 14: November 24, 1963 135
Chapter 15: Nixon, Watergate, Bell Mortgage, Costa Rica...
.... 148
Chapter 16: The Dating Game & A Family Affair 164
Chapter 17: Iran-Contra – The Summer Of 1987 174
Chapter 18: Castro Drug Lord 185
Chapter 19: Sociology, Dad, And Drug Lords 212
Chapter 20: Opie And Mayberry 223
Chapter 21: 1990's 228
Epilogue 241

Dedication

To Leanne and her family, Willie and his family, Maggie, Cori and Ian. To my husband, Chris, and our combined family members, with all my love.

Acknowledgment

I would like to thank my father, Guillermo Yglesias, first and foremost, for the candidness and stern guidance he gave me. To my husband and children who gave me the courage and support to write this book. My mother for her strength and honesty regarding this book and the others to follow. Most of all to all of my family and friends who have waited for this story.

"The role and importance of history is in how well it teaches us to use our own talents, take pride in our own history, love our own memories, and respect the history of others. To all those out there understanding and not destroying/rewriting history is the salvation of humanity".

About the Author

Cuba, News Year's Eve, 1958 changed the lives of all Cubans. It also changed the relationship between the island nation and the United States. The events of that night and those that came after it shaped the life of Crystina well before she was even born. She was born in Puerto Rico and raised throughout the Caribbean, South Florida, and California. Her childhood was a series of extraordinary events that would shape her life. This is about her childhood, her understanding of the world around her, and the incremental realization of her father's profession. How the age of the internet assisted her in verifying the information she knew and was told. How a child who was seen but never heard, until now.

Preface

A mom, a dad, two children, a dog, and a white picket fence – that's what the picture-perfect American family looks like. But that was not and is still not my family. If you think this is what this book is about, you might as well put it down now. This is not a book of fiction. These are my memories.

The characters in this book are real; their names and nicknames are theirs and even the places and experiences are real. The events that would shape my life primarily occurred decades prior to my existence.

It includes the Cuban struggle/war for independence from Spain (AKA the Spanish-American War), World War II, the rise of communism and socialism, and the rise of the United States as a global power. I wasn't even a glimmer in my parents' eyes when all of these events took place, yet they played major roles in my life.

In 1959, a talented young orator, a bearded attorney acting as a revolutionary, stole power in Cuba. Fidel Castro was able to capitalize on the two-class system that was Cuba; "the haves and the have nots." There really wasn't an in-between. The middle class in Cuba was just emerging. There was a huge disparity between the two classes making it a perfect situation for anyone to promise "change."

Fidel was in the right place at the right time. Make-no-mistake, as an attorney, he was a very talented orator. He promised "change." Fidel promised everyone would be equal and treated equally. Things that were already in place, such as, free education and a constitution, were promised. Cuba was to be independent and rely on no country, and no country would be its master, but Castro never said how he would achieve that. He just promised "change".." In short, he was selling a socioeconomic overhaul of the Cuban culture. The "haves" wanted more and wanted to pay less to the corrupt government, and the "have nots" wanted everything for nothing. Both classes backed the rich, bearded, fatigue-clad attorney in the Sierra Maestra Mountains of Cuba. Fidel disguised himself as a freedom fighter, but in the end, he was the ultimate capitalist. In doing so, he imprisoned an entire population and rendered them into slavery.

On December 31, 1958, my parent's world and that of the entire population "changed." The socialist government began to take form, and the "haves" soon realized the error in their ways. The United States, who also backed Fidel, soon began to realize this dark horse was a bad bet. Even Castro himself realized early on socialism would not work as his country could not sustain itself without the aid of others. He long considered The United States as the great evil empire responsible for the whoring of the Cuban island due to its capitalistic controlling ways. These political views were more aligned with communism than capitalism. Fidel Castro, the socialist, capitalized on his socialistic failure and aligned himself with Russia and communism. He exchanged one master for another.

Though he never saw himself as a capitalist, he turned out to be the ultimate capitalist. Castro, along with his family, and very few others, became the "haves," and the rest of the entire population were the "have nots." As the writing was on the wall, Cubans left the island in droves. The educated, and the wealthy fled. They fled with very little, for Castro had confiscated everything. My family was among the "haves" that fled when the bearded orator took control and stole an entire island.

Castro made formidable enemies both on the world stage and within my family. My family swore they would never allow their lives and that of their children to be stolen again. My family made careers out of ensuring this, hoping for retribution and reinstatement of their lives once Castro was removed. They all believed his tenure would be brief, and so did the United States.

I was born into this situation. A man I never met and I would never meet stole the lives of my family and shaped my life… a theft my family never forgave nor forgot. Memories are the most potent truth, and it is the purest form of history. These are my memories of how I became aware we were not the typical American family.

As the old English proverb goes, "Children are to be seen and not heard." Well, I was seen, and now I will be heard.

Chapter 1: You Know

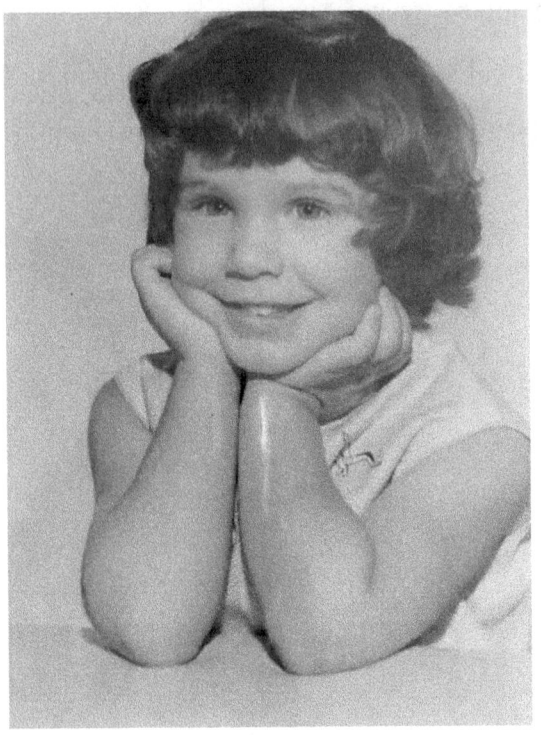

Okay, so I was not the girl next door. No, my dad was not Ward Cleaver, and my mother was definitely not June. The first twenty or so years of my life were not conventional. I think the closest my household came to "typical" was the first few years of my life. Now, when I say close, my context and your context may be on two different ends of the spectrum. My mom, being a housewife, was close to typical; that's it. Aside from that, nothing else was something that should be called 'typical.' Something was definitely different about us.

I have been asked a ridiculous amount of times, "When did you know?" Come on now, you just know. There was not a specific date or time. I guess the only answer is: I always knew! Let me put it into perspective. Throughout the different stages of growing up, I knew as much as I could comprehend. By the time I hit kindergarten, I had lived and traveled throughout the Caribbean and South Florida. I knew, okay?

In retrospect, the first clue was a trip to the Dominican Republic. I was about four years old, and my brother was two. He had fallen and split his head open. He was rushed to the nearest hospital in an ambulance with a police escort. I am sure that is how everybody gets rushed to the hospital in third-world countries. The two-year-old son of Cuban exiles is being whisked away like some diplomat's child. Hello – a clue! Oh yeah, while he was enjoying Mr. Toads' wild ride, I was left behind at the hotel with one of my Dad's "associates." At the age of four, you do not realize police escorts are not your everyday thing, not to mention having a grown-armed man for a babysitter. You do not think much of it. I now know he was a bodyguard, but then he was just Dad's "friend" who was there to entertain me.

As an oblivious preschooler, it never struck me as odd that the other preschoolers could describe what their dads did for a living, and all I knew was that he would be gone for days on end. The other dads went to work in the morning and came home at night. Not my dad. Had I comprehended the reality of exactly what he did at that age, it surely would not make for appropriate sandbox conversation.

My sheer bliss of oblivion would end in the summer of 1973. It was the summer before I was to begin kindergarten. My parents had planned a vacation to Spain. At least, that is how they sold the trip to me. This trip did not include children. So my parents left my brother and me in the care of our paternal grandparents.

My paternal grandparents were characters but were utterly unqualified to care for two small children. Especially when one of those children was me, a precocious, strong-willed, independent, and curious child, it was the perfect combination of characters for the scene that would unfold during my parents' absence...

Bless my grandparents' hearts, they did not stand a chance against my antics. The first few days of my parent's hiatus were uneventful. Somewhere around the third night, things changed dramatically. In the middle of the night, I woke up and could not go back to sleep. Trust me, not a good thing when you are a small child. As I crawled out of bed, I glanced out my window and saw a man sitting in a car directly across the street watching my house. I left my room and wandered through the house, grabbed a glass of water, and returned to my room. As I crawled back in bed, I looked out my window and saw the man was still there.

The following night, I waited in my room. Sleep was not on my mind. I was determined to stay awake to see if the man came back. Sure enough, he did. He parked himself in the same spot. I proceeded to make a game of his presence. Unfortunately, he was unaware of his role in this game. As a small child, I should have been scared of some stranger sitting in his car watching my house, but surprisingly, I was not afraid at all. Was I used to men watching over me – remember the Dominican Republic? Besides, I was curious. We all know where curiosity leads, but let's leave the cats out of this. As the night progressed, my new playmate knew that I was keenly aware of his presence. I mean, how could he not. I went from room to room, going to the windows and waiting for him to find me before I would move to another window. I was having a ball. So far, it was all an innocent and harmless game. It would all change the moment I upped the ante.

It was not good enough to go from room to room playing my version of hide-n-seek. Nope, I needed and wanted communication. Mind you, my house was wired. Yes, it had this lovely metal thing in the coat closet with lots of buttons that lit up. Nobody ever told me what it was; I was only told never to touch it. Ah, but children must be given specific and repetitive instructions. Something my parents did, but my grandparents forgot. Yes, they especially forgot the nighttime rule – "Do not open any windows or doors."

Well, hell, I was not touching the metal thing with the pretty lights. All I wanted to do was talk to my newly drafted playmate, who was across the street. How difficult could it be? All I had to do was open the window and call out to him…right? That is exactly what I did! I opened my bedroom window, and as I opened my mouth, the sound that blared out was not my voice but a loud shrieking alarm. My playmate was no longer sitting in his car. He was now running across the street toward the front door. I found out real quick that he was not alone. Apparently, he had a friend posted at the front door. I found out about him as he came through that door. That's right, all hell broke loose, and it was about to get a lot worse.

I was not sure what I had just done, but I sure as hell knew I was in some serious trouble. Not only had the loud alarm woke up everybody in the house, but also everyone within a one-mile radius of my house. My grandparents ran out of my parents' room screaming in Spanish. As if it weren't bad enough that a man had come bulldozing through the front door while a loud alarm continued shrieking, my grandparents were screaming, and police cars had now arrived. I thought that was it! I am going to jail, doomed to eat bread and drink water for the rest of my life.

As soon as the police arrived, my playmate excused himself and went outside to explain to the police what had happened – or at least that's what I thought was going on. As I watched him from my bedroom window, he made the police leave. Meanwhile, his buddy explained to my grandparents there was nothing to be afraid of and that I had set the alarm off. Finally, my playmate came back into the house and asked my grandparents to get me. Remember when I said I should have been scared of the stranger? Now I was petrified! I mean, this is the same man that made the police go away. What kind of stranger was he? The old adage, "be careful what you wish for," well, I was getting my wish, but I was the drafted playmate this time.

He told me not to be afraid. He introduced himself as Toni and explained he was there to watch over us at night while my parents were gone. No more games in the middle of the night. When I went to bed, I could wave to him from my window, and with that, he would know I was going to bed. Oh yeah, and absolutely under no circumstance was I to open a window or door unless it was an emergency. To be honest, the house could have caught fire, and I probably would not have opened one damn door or window after that night.

The following morning, not one word was said about the whole incident. Nothing was said by my parents when they returned from Spain. If there ever were one specific point in time that could be singled out when I knew, I would say that was it. It would be nine years later before I would find out the true nature of my parents' trip to Spain. As a five-year-old, I knew all I needed to know at the time, my family was definitely different.

The man in the car that was watching over us while our parents were away was "Uncle Toni." More about him later on in the book.

Chapter 2: The Child Of A Cuban Princess And A Caballero

So, we weren't the Cleavers, but we weren't the Munsters either. The best way to describe my family was more like Lucy and Ricky Ricardo with a twist. My mother, Lucy, wasn't a redheaded American housewife, but she was a Cuban housewife who found herself neck-deep in shit just like Lucy did all the time. My father, Ricky, was definitely every bit the Latin band leader except the band he played with, and their instruments were different than that of Ricky Ricardo's. My dad's instruments were of the military kind, say a cross between Ricky Ricardo and James Bond.

Yes, I am the offspring of these two characters. My childhood was completely different than theirs. Let's start with my mom, "the Cuban princess," here in the United

States; she would have been referred to as a "Debutante" – a "Cuban Princess" with all of its trappings. The announcement in the society page of her coming of age, official portraits, and let us not forget the extravagant society coming-out parties. Truly the equivalent of a Debutante!

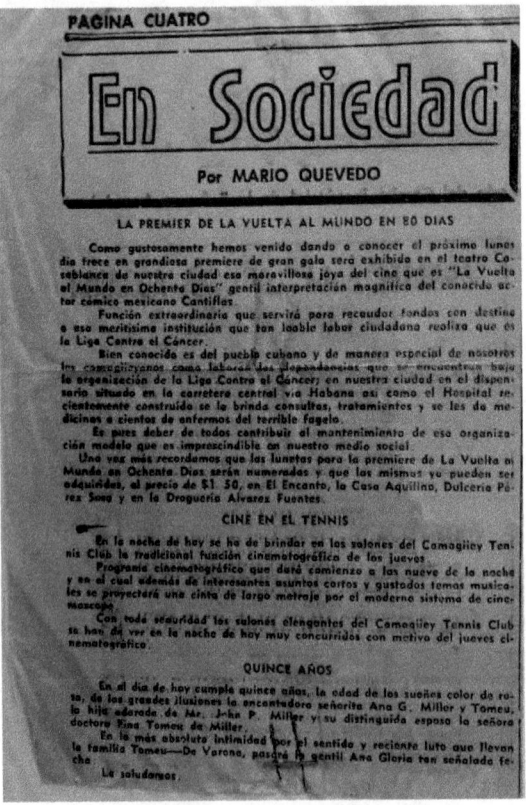

Cuban Newspaper announcing my mother's coming out

The daughter of aristocrats, an extremely wealthy Cuban family, she attended the best all-girls catholic schools in Camaguey, Cuba. She was raised by nannies in an era where children were seen and not heard. The oldest child of four, she was the apple of her maternal grandparents' eye. Though she was born into a very wealthy aristocratic Cuban family, her father – my grandfather – was an American. Yes, my mom was half and half. Cubans call that a Cortadito.

My mother, Ana Gloria Miller Tomeu formal coming of age portrait

Mom's life came to a screeching halt on December 31, 1958, when Fidel Castro took power. She landed in Miami sans her nanny, cook, and all the other niceties of her life back in Cuba. She went from a mansion to a three-bedroom house that housed up to 15 people at any one time during the first few years in Miami. A complete reversal of fortune it was!

Guillermo J Yglesias

Then there was my dad, "A Caballero," a gentleman. He was the son of an aristocrat and belonged to an extremely wealthy family as well. He attended the very best schools in Cardenas and Habana. As a child, he wanted for nothing. As he grew into a young man, he studied at the Cuban Naval Academy and became a naval engineer. He, too, would see his life and that of his family come to a screeching halt on that same fateful day in December 1958. Two life paths forever altered and never to be the same again.

How they met and how my mother arrived in Miami is another chapter, but how my father made it to Miami is really the beginning of half of this mess. You see, when Castro took over, all of the aristocratic, well-educated people fled. My father's family was no different. He was in the Cuban Merchant Marine at the time Castro upended his family.

In December 1960, his naval ship was in the Pacific heading to Asia, close to the Hawaiian Islands. He had just received word his family had finally made it to Miami safely. He had devised a plan to fake an appendicitis attack. A few officers on the boat were aware of his plan and helped him pull it off. They helped him jump ship.

Given the ship was not equipped to perform an appendectomy, he would have to be removed from the boat and taken to a hospital. The officers would have to call for medical assistance, which they did. The coast guard out of Honolulu responded to the medical emergency. An American Coast Guard Cutter was deployed to retrieve him from the Cuban Merchant Marine Ship. He was rushed to the hospital.

Upon arrival to the hospital, he was met by a doctor who had been alerted to his condition and impending arrival. Once he was alone with the doctor, my father explained to him about his family getting out, the plan to get him off the boat, and his desire to seek asylum. During his discussions with the doctor, he explained to him if he didn't have the surgery, the officers who helped him get off the ship would be facing prosecution, incarceration, or even execution. He was willing to have the surgery to keep them safe. The doctor agreed to perform the surgery, and the Cuban ship was notified my father would have to have an appendectomy. The ship would leave without him.

After the surgery, my father found himself in the recovery room with another man. He was a Korean war vet named Jim who had been injured during the war. His injuries required him to have follow-up surgeries. Jim and my father bonded while recovering from their respective surgeries. Jim would assist my father in establishing himself in Hawaii and getting asylum.

Cubans fleeing Cuba after Castro took over sought political asylum in the United States, typically through Miami. Unlike most Cubans, my father didn't come through Miami; he came through and requested Asylum in Hawaii. As he understood it, he was the second person to be granted political asylum there. The first person granted political asylum through Hawaii was in April 1960, the deposed South Korean President, Syngman Rhee. My father arrived in Miami at the end of 1961 and was recruited by a "few good men" right about the same time. He had one goal in mind; depose Castro.

My parents weren't any different than most people that fled Cuba early on; aristocratic, educated, and pissed off; their lives were stolen from them. Most, if not all of them came from families who built their fortunes from nothing.

They all thought their situation was temporary. In a few short years, they would all be back in their homes and resuming their lives in Cuba. They were all determined to make that happen at whatever cost. This was the mindset of all Cuban exiles in Miami in the 1960s.

To put things in perspective, during the pre-Castro revolution in Miami/Dade County, the Cuban population accounted for approximately 5% of the entire population. By 1970, that population had grown to just under 25%. I was born into this "American" demographic to parents who were born with silver spoons in their mouths, raised by nannies, and just like the rest of the Cuban population in Miami, determined to regain what was stolen from them. This was the recipe of my early life.

By the 1970s, most exiles had come to the realization they would never see their homeland again, and most re-made their lives here in the United States. Ricky and Lucy were no different. Lucy, the happy housewife, mother of two, was supporting Ricky in his chosen profession of fighting the good fight against Castro and Communism in this hemisphere.

Immediately after the 1959 Castro Revolution, around 200,000 Cubans fled the island to South Florida, primarily to the Miami Dade area. The early Cuban exiles were made up of the upper aristocratic and middle classes. These exiles were of European descent. Along with these Cuban exiles were several supporters of the ousted regime of Fulgencio Batista. Many exiles believed their situation was temporary since they also thought Fidel Castro would soon be toppled. During 1959 and the early part of 1960, travel between the United States and the stolen island country of Cuba was not heavily restricted.

In January 1959, Fidel was the world's darling; he was taking his victory lap and raising money for his "socialistic government." The world was watching to see what he would do, none more than the United States. They were already aware of his brother Raul Castro's communist leanings and feared Fidel would evolve in that direction. The United States took a watch-and-wait attitude. That changed on February 5, 1960, when Fidel Castro signed a trade treaty with the Soviet Union for 425,000 tons of sugar. President Eisenhower took that treaty as a signal.

As the relationship between the "Thief of Habana" and the United States deteriorated, travel to and from the seized island nation became more and more difficult. In a short period of time, Fidel came to the realization his socialistic utopia could not be financed with what little was left in Cuba. He could not reach out to the United States as this would mean his revolution failed, and he would be disgraced. Facing the rigors of running a country with no money and a less educated population to assist him, he quickly changed gears. In order for his revolution to survive, he, Fidel, went from socialist to communist almost overnight.

On January 3, 1961, President Eisenhower severed all ties with Cuba and closed the American Embassy in Habana. This diplomatic break was of no consequence to Fidel, but it was a huge consequence to Cubans still living on the island as they could no longer obtain visas. Instead of visas, Cubans now had to be admitted through the United States attorney general's parole authority.

In 1962, President Kennedy's administration enacted the Migration and Refugee Assistance Act. This act authorized assistance to a large number of Cubans fleeing Castro's Cuba seeking political asylum. There were two basic requirements for political asylum in the United States:

1) Asylum applicants had to establish that they fear persecution in their home country.

2) Applicants had to prove that they would be persecuted on account of at least one of the five following protected grounds: race, religion, nationality, political opinion, or particular social group.

Due to the nature of Cubans fleeing Castro's Communist Cuba, many immigration restrictions were specifically waived. The Immigration and Naturalization Service operated special processing centers in the Miami, Florida area. Newly arrived Cubans would be screened and held until they could be admitted into the United States. In 1962 the processing of Cuban immigrants was done in the "Freedom Tower" in Miami, Florida.

The Freedom Tower was the Ellis Island for the Cuban exodus. It was the beacon of light and hope. It housed The Cuban Assistance Center, offering nationally sanctioned relief to the Cuban exiles who sought political asylum from Castro's Cuba. A population transplanted to a new country. They had nothing, but they had their freedom and the will to fight Castro. This was the melting pot of South Florida throughout the 1960s.

Freedom Tower

Chapter 3: The Cuban Princess Flees Cuba

On New Year's Eve, December 31, 1958, the saying 'out with the old and in with the new' would have an inconceivable new meaning for all Cubans, including my mother. While lavish parties like the one at the Hilton Hotel and Casino in Habana were being held, cataclysmic events were unfolding during the last days of 1958. Approximately 173 miles east of Habana, the city of Santa Clara was under siege by the combined revolutionary forces, which defeated Batista's army. As all of these events unfolded, Fulgencio Batista fled the country to the Dominican Republic, forfeiting the island nation once known as the jewel of the Caribbean to those combined revolutionary forces.

Fulgencio Batista

As a fourteen-year-old, my mother had no idea of the ramifications of these events and how they would upend her life. Of course, she was aware of Castro and several other revolutionary groups attempting to usurp power. However, she was oblivious of the actions of those in her own immediate family that would set the stage for the flight from her home, community, and island. Her sheer lack of knowledge and that of her siblings to these actions would turn out to be their saving grace.

Che Guevara; "Butcher of La Cabaña"

On January 1, 1959, most Cubans found out about Batista's departure via a Radio address on "Radio Rebelde" from Fidel Castro. My family became aware within a few hours of his departure in the wee early morning hours. The news came to the house to warn my grandmother that her name was among the list of those that were to be rounded up, arrested, and taken to La Cabaña Fortress prison. Along with this news came the information that mass executions would begin immediately for all those found to be traitors, enemies of the state, spies, Batista military, and any member of the Batista regime. The writing was on the wall for my grandmother. It was just a matter of time.

My grandmother was among the very few women who practiced law in Cuba. She was a Cuban attorney no different than Fidel Castro. However, unlike Fidel, she also worked with a foreign government entity known as the CIA. The United States had maintained its fingers on the pulse of Cuba since the Spanish-American War (also known as the Cuban struggle/war for independence). She was a constitutionalist. Yes, Cuba had a constitution in place that resembled that of the United States in many ways. The combined revolutionaries, including that of Fidel Castro group, slapped together an interim government. Fidel and his group were the ones that took the lead. The masses recognized Fidel. By default, Castro became the leader of the combined revolutionary force.

The first rounds of arrests consisted of Batista military and regime members. These prisoners were taken to the Fortress to be dealt with by the "Butcher of La Cabaña, Che Guevara." On January 11, 1959, the province of Camagüey was taken over by the interim revolutionary government. By this time, the combined revolutionaries had taken control of all public transit. At all airports, soldiers were tasked with searches and interrogations. If they came across any persons on the list, they were detained and not allowed to leave the island.

José Miró

By February 16, José Miró Cardona, the prime minister of the interim government, was replaced by Fidel Castro. As things progressively got worse in Cuba, so did the rounding up, torture, and execution of those referred to by the interim government as "Escoria" (translation: human waste). There was uncertainty surrounding my family throughout 1959 and the first half of 1960. As the noose seemed to tighten around my grandmother's neck, a cable arrived from New Jersey informing the family that my grandmother's father-in-law was dying, and her husband needed to come quickly. An opportunity – a sad one, but one nonetheless.

Permission was requested to leave Cuba in light of this family emergency and it was granted but only for my grandmother and grandfather; the children were not allowed to accompany them. The children were the government's collateral, their assurance they would return. Sometime during the last days of May 1960 my grandmother and grandfather made their way to the airport in Camagüey. Along for the ride were my mother, her two younger brothers, and her maternal grandparents. My mother watched as her parents boarded a flight to Miami. Within hours of my grandparents' departure, my grandmother's law partner, Julio Santos Sordo, was taken into custody. My grandmother escaped the noose by mere hours.

Time Magazine cover of Jose Mira Cardona

Upon arrival in Newark, they were met by my grandfather's brother, General Edward Miller. En route to Old Bridge, my grandparents were peppered with questions from Edward regarding the children. Edward was livid with my grandparents for leaving the children behind. He explained that Cuba was operating under a Communist government, and history has shown one of the first things the communist do to the daughters of prominent figures is to defile, disfigure, or worse. He disclosed to them classified information regarding the daughters of those who had been executed had been tortured, defiled, disfigured, and some killed. The children had to get out immediately!

My grandparents had the opportunity to see my great grandfather but then immediately returned to Miami to plan the extraction of the children. This was a nightmare of staggering proportions. The clock was ticking, and every minute, hour, and day that passed, the children's fate could be sealed. One of the biggest obstacles was how to get the passport back to the kids in Cuba without my grandparents physically having to be the ones to do so. Then entered my grandmother's friend Irene. She was born and raised in Camagüey but resided in Miami and became an American Citizen. She was free to travel to and from without issue and was getting ready to do so.

Irene volunteered to take the passport and hand-deliver it to my mother. My grandmother gave the passport to Irene. Irene entered Cuba without issue, and she delivered the passport to my then sixteen-year-old mother. As one obstacle was removed, another one was raised – the exit visa. An exit visa had to be issued to my mother and her brothers under the passport by the interim Cuban government. A government that was holding them as preverbal hostages that they would release in exchange for the children's mother. The game of political football began along with the emotional rollercoaster that goes with it.

The passport was an American passport that was issued to my grandfather and his children. Why an American passport? Well, my grandfather was an American citizen posted in Cuba. My mother was born in Camagüey, along with her siblings. All three children were biologically my grandfather's kids, thus making them American citizens by birth. This was an international incident not unlike the future incident in 1993 involving Elian Gonzalez, a Cuban citizen but reversed. Here we had three American children being held by the interim Cuban government. The Cuban government denied the visas on the grounds they were minor children, and the parents had to present themselves in order to retrieve said children. In steps, the American consular agent based in Camagüey, Paul Tate.

Paul would now have to negotiate with the interim government for the release of the children. The second attempt came back with partial approval and denial. The interim Cuban government stated under Cuban law; the parents had to provide power attorney to my mother for the two minor boys to travel with her out of the country. Paul responded that these children are American citizens and American laws make no such requirement for them to travel with a power of attorney. The children must be released to travel out of the country to the United States. The interim government had no choice but to acknowledge the children were American citizens; therefore, jurisdiction falls under American law. The children were free to go…or were they?

On June 10, 1960, my mother and her two younger brothers, ages ten and four, were being driven to the airport in Camagüey by their maternal grandparents. Once the children said good-bye to their grandparents, not knowing if they would ever see them again, they were handed over into the custody of the American Consular Agent Paul Tate and what was described to me as the Airport Manager, William Patton. It must have been terrifying.

As the group entered the line for processing, the children were separated for questioning by Cuban officials. My mother and her youngest brother were taken into one room, accompanied by Paul Tate. The eldest brother was taken into another and was accompanied by William Patton. They would undergo questioning regarding their mother. They were repeatedly asked:

"Do you know Dr. Ana Matilda Tomeu de Varona?" – Answer: "No."

"Is your mother Ana Matilde Tomeu de Varona?" – Answer: "No."

Do you know Julio Santos Sordo? – Answer: "Yes."

"So, you know him, but you do not know Dr. Ana Matilde Tomeu de Varona?" – Answer: "Yes."

This questioning went on for hours. Finally, my mother lost her temper and told them, "Listen, Tomeu de Varona is my family's last name, but the family is huge, and I don't know all of them. My mother's name is Pina Miller Tomeu!" The official looked at her and said OK. He closed his questioning with, "You are going to meet your parents in Miami? My mother's response was, "Of course." With that, the children were reunited.

During the questioning, the plane had been held on the tarmac. They would be the last to board. They were escorted onto the tarmac by Paul Tate and William Patton. As they were saying good-bye, William Patton placed in my mother's hand a large capsule and said the following:

"Put this in your mouth under your tongue. Keep your mouth shut; the boys are to keep their mouths shut – I don't care how you do it; pinch them if you have to. There are men on this plane who are instructed if they hear anything out of your mouths regarding your mother they are to highjack the plane and return it to Habana. You will be greeted by airport officials give them that capsule. Do you understand?" She nodded her head, kissed him good-bye, and boarded the plane.

There she was on the plane with two small boys surrounded by people she did not know, and among them were some men who meant to keep them from their parents.

As the plane taxied down the runway, she had no idea she would not return to Cuba for sixty years. Now all she had to do was hold it together for the next 90 minutes. My mother has flown cross country and into Europe, but she said this flight was the longest of her life.

The plane arrived on the tarmac in Miami, where all passengers disembarked. As the children were traveling as unaccompanied minors, they were greeted by airport officials and were removed from the line. Upon entering the building, my mother handed the official the capsule. Unbeknownst to her, the paper in that capsule was a list. On that list were the names of three men who were passengers on that same flight. These were the men tasked with returning the plane back to Cuba had she or her siblings made any reference to their mother. Those men were then removed from the line of passengers and arrested.

As the children worked their way through immigration, they could see their parents awaiting them. Upon exiting immigration, the Cuban princess, my mother, found a new life awaiting her far from the life she once knew. A life with an uncertain future.

Armed Rebels fighting in Santa Clara, Cuba

On December 31, 1958, the City of Santa Clara fell to the combined efforts of several different revolutionary forces, including that of Fidel Castro; Che Guevara's forces. Fidel was planning the action against the City of Santiago all the while most Cubans outside of Cuba celebrated New Year's Eve quietly. In Habana and its suburbs, there were several lavish parties attended by tourists, diplomats, aristocrats, and members of the Batista regime. However, Batista celebrated New Year's Eve at Camp Columbia, the headquarters of the Cuban army.

12/29/1958: Rebel group derails and captures "El Tren Blindado" (armored train), Santa Clara, Cuba

Batista boarded a plane to the Dominican Republic with a handful of about 40 people consisting of family, friends, and advisors. This was not a chaotic flight; it was very well planned. For months he was draining accounts and moving accounts for his life in exile. All was in place. Once everything was secured and the tide had turned in favor of the combined revolutionary forces, the decision was made to flee. He shared his decision on New Year's Eve with a select few, his closest advisors giving them a few days if not hours to flee themselves. Thirty-five minutes into the new year, Batista was gone.

Within minutes of the plane leaving the tarmac, rumors spread of his flight from power. As the rumors spread via shortwave radio throughout the island, Batista's allies fled by any and all means necessary; plane or yachts. Batista allies were not the only ones on the move due to these rumors. Batista was gone, but the war within revolutionary factions was just beginning. The race was on to fill the vacuum of power that existed.

Carlos Franqui, Radio Rebelde

By the time Castro was informed of Batista's flight, events had been set in motion. The head of Radio Rebelde, Carlos Franqui, took to the airwaves and filled the void over the radio that emerged in the absence of the government. Castro wanted to fill that void as quickly as possible he made his way to the town of Palma Soriana to record radio broadcasts.

Castro was furious he felt betrayed and was fearful his group would be shut out. So he took to the airwaves to declare victory. He wasted no time and acted swiftly. The propaganda machine was in full force, with the masterful silver-tongued orator in full control of the message. That message was: he and his forces had won the victory for the people.

Fidel Castro, Radio Rebelde

The forfeiture of Cuba was comprised of multiple revolutionary groups coming together to fight for a common cause even if they did not agree with each other politically and the United States suspension of military aid to Batista. The claim that Castro and his group were some great military minds that ousted Batista is a fable. It was Castro oratory skills and propaganda which gave the forfeited prize of Cuba to him.

The first wave of Cubans fleeing Cuba was not the educated, aristocrats, and wealthy landowners. It was those part of and or associated with the Batista regime. Their window of opportunity to flee was a mere eight days. Once Castro reached Habana, the mass arrests began, followed by mass executions. They began with those known and assumed Batista associates, military, and figureheads.

Execution at La Cabaña Fortress prison of Jose Rodriguez

On January 4, 1959, Che Guevara left the City of Santa Clara to take up his new appointment as the Commander of La Cabaña Fortress prison. On the days prior to his appointment, he ordered 25 people to be executed, some of which he did himself. He would reign over La Cabaña

Fortress as judge, jury, appellate court, and executioner until November 26, 1959. In that time, he earned the name the "Butcher of La Cabaña." He has been quoted gloatingly:

Execution in La Cabaña (photo taken from The Nuevo Herald)

"'Fusilamientos' (executions by firing squad), yes, we have executed, we execute, and will continue executing while necessary." Even after his departure from La Cabaña, he still ordered the executions that took place there. To this day, there is no formal count of those ordered to be executed by Che; from as little as one hundred to thousands, the true figure shall never be known.

1959 was a turbulent and dangerous time. It would take Fidel 45 days to officially take control of the island and name himself prime minister of the interim government. In order to keep control of the people, they had to be scared into submission, both by the interim government and the use of mob rule. This was done by intimidation and cancel culture. The first to feel this wrath were those who failed to make it out on the first wave of exiles.

Los Barbudos

This tactic was to kill as many as possible who were associated with, had ties to, had worn police or military uniform under the Batista regime whether they were guilty of anything or not. Heavily armed groups of bearded soldiers known as "Los Barbudos" were tasked with apprehending them and anyone they saw fit to condemn. They made sure those apprehended were beaten, preferably with as many witnesses as possible so the word would spread and so would the fear. There were no records kept of those who died during these beatings. Along with these actions was the ongoing struggle to attain and keep power by Fidel Castro.

He subscribed to the saying "keep your friends close but your enemies closer." True to this mindset, he appointed several competing revolutionary forces leaders to positions within the interim government. If their popularity grew or if they swayed in any way against the propaganda, they mysteriously died or were imprisoned.

On October 28, 1959, Camilo Cienfuegos died in a mysterious plane crash just days after arresting Huber Matos. Matos was another revolutionary leader who became disillusioned with Fidel and the communist infiltration of the government. He felt the revolution had betrayed the island and its people. He would be tried for treason, sentenced to 20 years in a Cuban prison. This was the reality of Cuba in 1959.

Dr. Ana Matilda Tomeu de Varona

This was also the reality for my Grandmother, Dr. Ana Matilde Tomeu de Varona, aka Dr. Ana Matilde Miller Tomeu aka Pina Tomeu, aka Pina Miller Tomeu. Obviously, all are one and the same. Within the Cuban culture, then as it is now, everyone has a nickname. The nickname is what your family and friends know you by, not your legal name. My grandmother's nickname was Pina. Her children only knew her by that name. So when government officials asked them about a woman with all those other names, the children had no clue who they were referring to. It saved them and allowed them to flee. Others were not as lucky: Julio Santos Sordo received a 30-year sentence. After serving ten-plus years, he would be released and flee the island with his family. He eventually ended up in Glendale, California, and lived out the remainder of his life there. William Patton would be executed in 1961 as a CIA spy and an enemy of the state. As for Paul Tate, he returned to the mainland. He died on July 5, 1983, in Florida.

William Patton

"World News Briefs" section announces the execution of William Patton in Cuba.

Chapter 4: Lost & Found

There were several family members around, obviously including my paternal and maternal grandparents, aunts, uncles, cousins – you know the whole bit. Yes, I had my personal Cuban exile community. We all lived within minutes of each other in Miami, with the exception of my paternal grandparents. Most of my memories were of spending time with family members.

My home was one block away from my elementary school. When I became of age, my life settled down. I went to school like everybody else. If you had seen me with my class, you'd agree I did not look any different than other children because I was not different. If you haven't figured it out by now, "I" was not what made our family different. It sure was not the fact we were Cuban Exiles. In those days, the entire population of Miami could make that claim. What made my family different was my father – to be exact, his chosen profession.

Before I began grade school, I lived throughout the Caribbean and South Florida. I was a well-traveled child. I was not an army brat, well, not really. I guess I can better be called a government brat. I am not sure what the government would have called me; nevertheless, I will say there were and are several more like me out there.

Anyway, kindergarten went by uneventfully and so did most of the first grade. However, toward the end of first grade, I found out we were moving. We were not moving down the street; we were moving to Costa Rica; we were moving to Central America! I don't remember how it was explained or even if it was explained to me.

It was not until I was thirteen years old when I overheard a conversation when I found out why we had to move to Costa Rica. I forgot to mention, along with curiosity comes eavesdropping. To move is something I would categorize under free will. You choose to go – a far cry from ejection, like Billy Martin, the manager of the New York Yankees, who would piss off the umpires and would be EJECTED from the game. He did not want to leave the game but was forced to. Well, the long and short of it was my father was EJECTED from the good ole U.S.A.

That's right, he was "asked to leave." Why? That's a good question to ask right about now. You see, my father and some "associates" were running government and privately funded operations from the Florida Keys to Cuba. They were running guns to the rebels to overthrow Castro. You see, the United States, after its very public attempt and humiliating failure to overthrow Castro in the "Bay of Pigs," was still at it in private. Except for this time, it was a bit different; if you were caught even by your own government, they would not acknowledge you. My dad was the exception as he was the only one that walked away from a covert operation gone bad, but that's another story, another chapter.

For his role, he was asked to leave the United States. So, the exile was exiled yet again? Not really; just re-assigned to Central America to fight Castro. To be exact, to fight Castro's influence in the region, specifically Nicaragua. So, my younger brother and I were packed up and shipped out to Costa Rica. It was a very precarious time in Central America. Fidel Castro was funding and providing armaments to the Sandinista revolutionaries in Nicaragua.

Anastasio Somoza Debayale
President of Nicaragua 1967-1979

The spread of Castro's policies through Central America was not in the best interest of the United States. Although the president of Nicaragua at that time, Anastasio Somoza Debayle, was a dictator, he was an American ally who had the support of the United States from the infancy of

Nicaragua to the insurgency of the Sandinistas. My father's assignment was to quash the insurgency of the Sandinistas in Nicaragua at whatever cost.

Tronco Negro Ranch; From left to right - Loli, Beatrize, Tio Julito, Tia Ana Louisa

Of course, as a seven-year-old child, I had no idea of the political and legal reasons behind our move. All I was told was that we were moving to Costa Rica to be closer to my father's work and my mother's uncle's family. Though most of our family was in Miami, my mother's maternal uncle (Tio), Julio, and his family lived in San Jose, the capital of Costa Rica, and had a ranch on the outskirts of San Jose, Tronco Negro. For the first few months, we resided in a very nice hotel in Punta Arenas. During the week, we would be at the hotel, but on weekends, we would stay at the family ranch. My dad usually met us at the ranch. For a child, it was paradise; there were horses, cattle, iguanas, parrots, and monkeys.

From left to right Willie, Beatrize, Loli, and me

Those first few months in Costa Rica felt like one very long vacation. My brother and I wandered through the hotel by ourselves like we owned the place. The reality was, there was always someone watching us. If my mother was not with us (and even when she was) there was always one of Dad's associates nearby. Days were filled with swimming, chasing iguanas, ordering room service, sitting at the bar, and driving the hotel van. Unfortunately, like all vacations, it all came to an end. That's right; it was time to enroll in school.

First, we moved into Tio Julio's apartment in San Jose, which made it easier for my mother to deal with my father's absence. Tio Julio had two young daughters, Beatrize, age 9, and Loli, age 4, which made this move easy on my brother and me. We had instant playmates. We all stayed in the apartment during the week, and on the weekends, we would go to the ranch, where we would meet Julio and my dad.

The girls attended traditional private Costa Rican Schools, which I was hoping I would attend so as not to be alone, but that was not to be. I was enrolled in the American school, Lincoln. Lincoln School was a cross-section of kids consisting of diplomat, foreign, and military-affiliated children. It was a secure campus boosting armed guards. In fact, if you visit the school today, you will be greeted at the front gate at the guard shack with guards armed with AK-47's.

As the first day of school drew near, my dad came home to the apartment. It was going to be a big day for me. I was happy he was there. I was starting a new school in a new country, at least that is what I thought of that day. However, children are the last to know how the planned events of the day would unfold.

I don't remember much of what happened during the actual school day except that I was pulled out of the class along with other kids and led to the cafeteria to meet our bus driver. The bus driver introduced herself and called out our names. Once she completed her roll call, she gave us instructions. The next time she called our names, we were to give her our address. Well, when she called my name, I gave her the only address I knew: my address in Miami. Everyone laughed. She told me it was okay and that she had my address. Okay? I had never ridden a bus with my parents, let alone by myself, and this lady that I had just laid eyes on was telling me it was going to be okay? Once she got all the information needed, we were all instructed to meet back in the cafeteria when school let out.

I did as I was told. I went to the cafeteria and was then led to the bus. As the bus traveled through the streets of San Jose, I did not recognize any of the landmarks that I was familiar with to Tio Julio's apartment. I began to pay very close attention to all the other kids. As the bus made its stops, the bus driver called out the student's name that were to disembark. I would watch the students at the stop walk in different directions at each stop.

Then it was my turn. My name was called. I stood up and walked to the front of the bus. The bus driver said this was my stop. I told her this was not my house and not where I lived. She laughed and replied, "Yes, I know your house is in Miami." She asked me to step out of the bus. I began to cry. She again told me to step out of the bus. I did what I was told.

I found myself in front of an apartment building I had never seen before. I was alone in a foreign country, and I had no idea where I was. I sat on the front stoop of the apartment building and began to cry. Several men came out of the building, which made me much more frightened. One of the very last men that came out tried to speak with me to find out what was wrong. I was petrified. My instincts told me to run, and I was getting ready to when a lady came out. She must have recognized that I was scared out of my mind. She must have known the man trying to talk to me, or at least she spoke to him as she did. Upon her request, he backed away from me so that she could find out what was going on.

The lady approached me and asked me why I was crying. I blurted it out. I must have been talking a million miles an hour in between sobs. "I had been dropped off by the bus driver," I said. I told the bus driver I did not live here. The lady looked at me and said that I was right; I did not live there, but the question was, where did I live? She asked the infamous question; yep, that's right! What was my address? And yep, again, my answer was the same. I gave her my address in Miami. She stood back, and as she did, her young daughter came out of the building.

Her daughter was about my age and was asking her mom what was going on and why was I crying. Her mother explained the dilemma. Finally, the lady asked me where and with who I was staying within Costa Rica. Eureka! Finally, here was a question I could answer: "Tio Julito's apartment."

It meant the world to me; I figured everybody knew who he was and where he lived, right? Wrong. The lady realized I had no idea what Tio Julito's address was.

She began to ask me questions regarding landmarks, realizing I knew how to navigate by landmarks. She asked if I wanted her to take me to Tio Julito's apartment. *Yes, yes, dear God. Yes!* I thought.

"I know what you are thinking. A seven-year-old, alone in a foreign country, dropped off and left, was now going to get into a stranger's car. Didn't your parents not teach you not to talk to strangers and never to get in a stranger's car?"

Yes, they did, but what else was I to do?

I climbed in her car with her daughter. She began driving San Jose by the landmarks as I had described to her. I stopped crying. I could see familiar places. I was actually going to the right place. Finally, she pulled up to the building and asked me if that was the right building. I said yes. She said she would watch me go into the building before leaving.

I got out of her car and ran into the building. As she pulled away, I ran down the hallway until I got to the door. I knocked on the door and screamed, "It's me; I'm home." Nothing. I banged on the door. Nothing. I kicked the door and screamed, "I'm home from school." Still nothing. Nobody was home.

How could that be? How can nobody be home? Did they not know what time school got out? I went from scared to downright pissed. One thing was for certain; I was not moving from that door until someone got home.

There was a perfectly good explanation why nobody was home; they were out looking for me. Every parent's nightmare, right? A child has gone missing. Now compound that with my father's profession. It quickly went from missing, to kidnapped, being held for something in return. The alarm was sounded, and everybody from family members to my father and his "associates" were out looking all over San Jose.

Ultimately, my parents called the school and confirmed that I was on the bus, and the stop I was dropped off at was the correct drop-off point. I know what you are thinking; how could that have been the correct drop-off point? It was not Tio Julito's apartment building. Unannounced to me, my parents decided the first day of school would be a great day to move into their new apartment. Yes, they gave the school the new address but forgot to tell the minor child of this minor change in her life!

The drop-off point was the apartment building right next door to my parent's apartment building. My father immediately went there and found a few of the men that were around when I had been there. They told him I was crying hysterically and that I would not speak to them. They told him of the lady in the building who not only spoke with me but took me in her car. As the search for me continued, my father waited in the front of the building until the lady returned with her daughter.

My father questioned her about my whereabouts. When she realized that he was my father, she immediately told him where he could find me. She apologized and told him that I had no idea they had moved today and that I told her I lived at my mother's uncle's house. My father thanked her and left.

I sat in front of that door for hours. Finally, someone showed up. It was my dad. He scooped me up in his arms and held on to me. He had tears in his eyes. I, of course, oblivious to everything that had happened, was still very upset that nobody had been home to greet me when I got home from school, and I let him know. He chuckled and led me out of the building and into his car.

That evening he came into my room to say goodnight as he tucked me in and gave me my Mrs. Beasley doll to sleep with; he spoke to me of the dangers of the day. He told me someone should have told me of the move and assumed someone had. My father told me that night that there are many people out there that would do anything to hurt him and even me, my brother, and my mother to get to him. That night was the night that I became fully aware of my surroundings. It was the beginning of my awareness of everything and everybody around me and the end of a carefree childhood.

Chapter 5: A Night To Remember

After my eventful first day of school, I can honestly say the remainder of my educational career in Costa Rica was quite normal. Homework, schoolyard antics, and the occasional bringing home of some stray animal (the latter of these my mom was never particularly keen on). Sometime during this school term, my parents moved again, and yes, I was absolutely informed.

I remember the first time I saw the house. It was beautiful with a red tile roof and white plaster walls. I walked into the house and found it breathtaking; it had dark mahogany floors. My favorite part of the house was the aviary. It was full of small tropical parakeets. When you walked through the front door, it was the first thing you saw.

Toni Iglesias

The house was sparsely furnished. All of our furniture from Miami was still in shipping containers somewhere at large. It was a three-bedroom home. My brother and I shared a bedroom. Both our beds were set up on the floor. My mom and dad had their own room. The third bedroom, however, was a bit of a surprise. It belonged to Tio Toni? Yeah, Toni was as much of a surprise as the macaw that roamed the house. Don't get me wrong; I knew who Toni was. He was an "associate" of my father who I had met in Miami; he was my playmate in the car parked across the street from my house. Actually, his second wife and two children spent quite a bit of time with us the last twelve months we were in Miami. However, he was now in Costa Rica, but without his family, and now he was my uncle?

I remember making a comment about Toni and my father saying he had the same last name (spelt differently), and that's it; that was all that was ever said. Tio Toni came with a new woman, Ana. So, we were just one big happy family under one big red tile roof. My father and Toni would go to work together and come home together. Yep, that's right, Toni was no different than my dad. They would be gone for days and would be home for days. I'm sure Costa Rica must have been some sort of refuge from Nicaragua's hostile environment, the political reality, and the gruesome work. The home must have been their sanctuary.

Despite it all, I thoroughly enjoyed Costa Rica. My mother, on the other hand, did not. I don't think anybody could blame her. She was in a foreign country, thousands of miles away from her family with two kids, and married to the Cuban version of James Bond. How enjoyable could that have been? I mean, every time your husband, the father of her children, steps out the door, there is a good possibility he may never return. Now that screams stability. Mom would eventually blow up months later.

My mom had enough a few days after I witnessed something I should have never seen. To this day, I am not sure if that was the final straw or what. I have never spoken about this with either of my parents. In fact, I don't think my father ever knew I was awake that night, and I saw the whole thing. After the whole bus incident and my dad's conversation with me that same evening, I had become more astute of my surroundings and all of the ongoings that affected my world.

My father typically worked late, and my mom would put us to bed and simply tell us Dad was coming home late that night. I would lay in bed and wait. I waited until my brother was asleep and my mother was in bed before I got up and roamed the house. I was far more cautious roaming this house than the house in Miami. I would normally go to the front living room and wait to see the headlights shine through the window when dad and Toni got home. I'd peek out the window to make sure it was them, then run back to my room, hop in bed, and pretend I was asleep. Whether I fooled anybody, I don't know; all I knew was my dad was coming through the door to kiss my brother and me good night before he went to bed with mom.

I had done this several times, and nothing unusual ever happened. Well, there is always a first time for everything. I snuck out of my room as usual and went to the front room. Everything that usually happened had occurred up until I peeked out the window.

I watched my dad and Toni get out of the car as usual. As I was getting ready to turn and run back to my room, a man came out of nowhere and approached my dad and Toni. A discussion began, and from the tone in my dad's voice, I knew he was not glad to see this man. I couldn't help but keep watching. The discussion continued, and the man was expressing himself using his hands, so much so that Toni grabbed the man's hands at one point. My father then ordered the man to leave.

I remember the man chuckled and made a comment that he would leave but added that he would be back, and maybe next time, my dad may not be the one at home. The tone in all of their voices changed dramatically. I couldn't hear very much after that. They were speaking in low tones. It lasted a few minutes, then all of a sudden, there was a popping sound and a flash of light. I watched as the man hit the ground. I couldn't move.

I watched as Toni picked the man up and loaded him in the trunk of the car. My father grabbed the water hose and washed down the driveway. Then they pulled away. I stood there watching, trying to reconcile what I had just seen. After getting my wits about me, I went back to my room, crawled into bed, and pulled the sheets over my head. I lay in my bed just thinking about what my dad had told me months before as it echoed in my head: "There are many people out there that would do anything to hurt him, including hurting me, my brother, and my mother to get to him." This man must have been one of them.

The following morning when I awoke, I found my mother in the kitchen getting breakfast ready. She told me to be very quiet and said that "Papi" had gotten in extremely late the previous night and that he was still sleeping. I didn't say a word. I just nodded my head yes in acknowledgement of her request. I went out in the front yard and stood right where the man had been. There was nothing, not one sign of what had happened the night before.

A few days later, I witnessed my mother have a meltdown. My father and my mother were arguing. She was crying, and I can remember her telling him she could not take it any longer. She did not like living in Costa Rica. She did not like being alone, left alone with two children while he was out gallivanting, saving one third-world country at a time. She told him she had had enough and was taking my brother and me and going back home.

I don't think they knew I was there and heard most of their argument. I don't know if the argument began with my father telling her about the man from the other night or what. All I knew was that my mother was done. She could not take any more of it. I watched as she rushed around the house packing. The suitcases were packed into our green Chevy Nova along with anything else she could fit into the car. She even packed these multi-colored clothes' hamper she had brought with us from Miami. Once she felt she had everything, she collected my brother and me and led us out the door.

As we approached the car, my father was there and said, "How far do you really think you are going to get by yourself with two small children." She told him she did not know, but she could no longer live there, and she was going to do her best to get home. I was placed in the back seat, on top of suitcases. I was as high as the rear window, and I had to lay down to fit. My brother was in the front seat. As we pulled away, I watched the house and my dad fade in the distance.

The house faded into the distance, and so did Toni. After that date, I never saw him again. In the early '90s, my mom went on her annual Miami trip, and while out and about, she ran into Toni. He wanted to get together with her and his wife "Ana" for dinner. My mother mentioned it to my grandmother, who said that was a bad idea based on information she had about Toni's then business dealings.

Chapter 6: Road Trip 1976

Children are amazing creatures; they can literally fall asleep in a matter of minutes being placed in a car. The moment my dad and the house were out of sight – that's right, I fell asleep. I woke up somewhere near the border of Costa Rica and Nicaragua, and waking up, I felt like I missed some really big event because my father was now behind the wheel of the car.

Don't get me wrong, I was happy that my dad was with us. I knew that with him, we would make it home. From the conversations my parents had, my dad had met up with my mom at Punta Arenas. Anyway, I had a back seat view of Central America on this road trip.

Like any other child on a road trip, I asked the most annoying question: "When are we going to get there?" I did that a few times. When it finally got on my parents' last nerve, I got that "look." Even though my family was different than your typical all-American family, we all know that look. You know the one, the one you get when you ask that question one too many times, and the look you get is, "Ask it one more time, and I'll knock you into next year," kind of look. So now, I was a quiet observer with a window to the world from the back window of our green Chevy Nova.

As we drove through Nicaragua, I noticed the children. There were so many of them in the streets. They were ill-kept. Throughout the entire country, I saw such poverty. Side by side with poverty were armed men. Some were government officials, but most were peasants. It was now crystal clear exactly what my dad meant when my mom pulled away from the house. There was no way we would have made it home.

As we passed through different areas, the car would be stopped, and my dad exited the car. I would watch when I was awake that my dad had brief conversations with some armed man and then return to the car, and we would pull away. This happened time and again through Nicaragua and Honduras. As we were going through Honduras, my parents began talking about stopping in El Salvador to see my dad's aunt, Lucrecia.

My parents' discussions even hinted that we would stay for a few days. Hot Damn! I didn't know who this Lucrecia was, and to be honest, I really did not care. All I knew was I was getting out of the car and off those suitcases. We arrived in El Salvador during the first few days in February. My father pulled up to a house, and we got out.

As we approached the house, his cousin Lucri met us at the door. She seemed to be happy to see us. It was a large house, wood floors, and a large beautiful courtyard. I was a bit confused for a moment but that was until I found her. I wandered through the house, exploring... well, exploring without permission. Don't all kids do that? I wandered into a room where this elderly woman was lying in a bed. She was dressed in white, had white hair, a fair complexion, and wrinkles! I remember thinking to myself that she was older than dirt. I don't think I had ever met someone that old; not even my great grandparents looked that old. I dared not vocalize my thoughts because it would be considered being rude, and boy would I have been knocked through the wall for such comments.

Within a few minutes, my father and his cousin, Lucri, found me. Apparently, I had found Lucrecia, my dad's aunt and Lucri's mother. I was formally introduced to my grand aunt. As the minutes passed, yet another family member that I had never met came out of the woodwork. It was Lucrecita, Lucri's daughter. There must have been a serious naming shortage with that side of the family because every female in that household had the same name.

Lucrecita was in her late teens or very early twenties; she would be both mine and my brother's lifesaver during the few days we were in El Salvador. My parents checked into a very nice hotel during our stay. The next day Lucrecita came to the hotel and took my brother and me swimming. Later that day, she asked permission to take me out to eat. She took me to a Salvadorian restaurant where she ordered "Pupusas."

As I sat in this restaurant, I watched the different types of people. There were primarily two different types; European-looking individuals and short, dark-skinned individuals. Lucrecita observed me as I was studying the differences. She tried her very best to explain to a second-grader the difference between the two, back to the Pupusas. As a child, that name for food does not strike you as 'Umm yummy!' You instead associate it with poo because of the name.

When our order arrived, the Pupusas looked like some round-looking Empanada (a form of meat pie). I watched Lucrecita break one and take a bite. It was filled with cheese. I was really happy it had nothing to do with poo and was actually very good. That night in bed at the hotel, I realized people are different, and so is the food.

The following morning when I awoke, my mom had already gotten up and left the room with Lucrecita, and my father was still asleep. Every child has an innate instinct: survival! If a child wishes to survive, they must adhere to rule number one; never wake up a sleeping parent! So, my brother and I played very quietly in our bed for a while with his Hot Wheel car.

We rolled the car up and down the bed, then the car fell off and rolled underneath it. It was very dark in the room, and we could not see the car. My brother was deathly afraid of the underneath of any bed, so that left me to retrieve the car. I needed some sort of light in order to find it, and turning the light on in the room with my sleeping father was out of the question. As I glanced around the room, my father's gold cigarette lighter came into view. *Ah-ha! A light source!* I thought. I crawled out of bed and grabbed the lighter. I positioned myself at the foot of the bed and lit the lighter to see where the car had gone. "Found it!" I grabbed the car and closed the lighter.

Adults should never leave small children alone to entertain themselves. When they do, it seems to end up in some huge mess. The pretty lighter had captured our attention; we were mesmerized. My, my, what could we do with this pretty lighter? Burn something! Wait a minute; burn means fire, and we were told not to play with fire. So, the next thought was, *what puts a fire out?* Water...and the hotel room had a bathtub.

My brother and I snuck out of our bed and into the bathroom, closing the door behind us so as not to wake the sleeping parent. We had a lighter and a bathtub, but what to burn? Toilet paper! Yes, my brother and I filled the bathtub full of toilet paper. No, we didn't just throw rolls in; we unrolled the toilet paper and dumped it into the bathtub. Once we ran out of toilet paper, we lit the lighter and then the toilet paper. At first, my brother and I were in awe of the pretty color, but after a bit, we realized it was time to put the fire out. That "time" came as the wax shower curtain began to melt. Though water definitely puts out fires, the one thing children do not realize is that when you first add water, the flames roar up before going out. Pretty damn scary for two small children!

Remember when I said children have certain instincts, like survival? Well, we threw that out the window and called for my sleeping father. The poor man, half asleep, wandered into the bathroom in his underwear to be greeted by his two adoring children and a bathtub on fire. He began screaming in Spanish and English…let's say Spanglish. All I could make out was "Estos niños think que soy un pedaso de Kentucky fried Chicken;" that is Spanglish for "these damn kids think I'm a piece of Kentucky fried chicken." Timing is everything, so they say. Right at that moment, my mother, Lucrecita and some man came through the door.

Lucrecita grabbed my brother and me and took us into the hall while my father turned the water on and killed the fire. All the while, he was going on and on to my mother about how he has been shot at, chased off roads, faced death several times at the hands of others, and his own damn children tried to cook him like some chicken. Once everything calmed down, we were brought back into the room and punished…well, sort of. The punishment was to be grounded to the hotel room, but Lucrecita quickly and sarcastically pointed out that was brilliant – grounding children to the hotel room that they set on fire because they were bored! She instead volunteered to take us swimming. My father reluctantly agreed. It was going to be our last day there, and we would soon be locked up in the car and back on the road.

Chapter 7: Guatemala

It was the early morning of February 4, 1976. Big deal, right? Damn straight it was. I was shaken awake, literally. No, nobody was shaking me to wake me up. The whole room was shaking! I was smack dab in the middle of my first earthquake.

It seemed like a scene out of an "I Love Lucy" episode. I woke up to find my bed moving back and forth away from the wall. I looked toward my parents' bed and saw my mom hanging onto the headboard mounted to the wall while her bed moved out from under her and away from the wall like mine. She was not only hanging onto the headboard, but she was screaming.

Every stick of furniture in the room was moving. It felt like the room shook forever. Just as it started, it stopped. When it stopped, my mother jumped out of bed and began saying; we are out of here! Let's go! Get up; we are leaving! She ran around the room like Lucille Ball did in every episode of her show.

We all got up, got dressed, and quickly packed our things. We exited the room and went down the stairs. As we entered the lobby, we found it in shambles with furniture tossed around, plaster falling off walls and the ceiling, people running in and out of the building, and some looting things from the lobby. Little shakes kept rocking underneath our feet. With every shake, my mother screamed louder! We found our car, loaded it, and left. I was returned to my back seat hovel. That hovel gave me a first-hand view of the devastation caused by an earthquake. Apparently, the earthquake's epicenter was in Guatemala, and we still had to drive through Guatemala.

As we drove through El Salvador and Guatemala, I saw towns completely leveled by the quake, dead bodies, children, and armed people in the streets robbing and looting. My father never stopped, not once.

All the way through those countries, my mother kept going on about the quake and how she would rather deal with a hurricane than to ever have to deal with another one of those earthquakes. I had to agree. It really wasn't the most pleasant experience of my life. What was worse was seeing everything after it.

The aftermath of a devastating earthquake is chaos, looting, and violent crime. I may have been a grade-schooler, but I knew things were very dangerous by watching my father. His gun was on his lap, and he was very uneasy. There were several times he would avoid stop points and find his way around them. We did not stop at any checkpoints in that country. All the while, I had a back seat view of a devastated population. It was sad and scary all at the same time, and unlike TV, I couldn't change the channel or turn it off.

My brother and I had both our parents, a car, and we were leaving that place while so many others had no way out. Being locked up in the car was not so bad now. I stayed awake for a long time, but eventually, I could not fight the urge to close my eyes. When I awoke, we were in Mexico.

We stopped in Mexico and had breakfast. We entered the restaurant and sat down. My father ordered for all of us. When he ordered, he did not order milk or juice for my brother and I, he ordered Coca-Cola. I looked at him like he'd lost his mind. I asked him why. He said, "We are in Mexico, and we do not drink the water." He also said he did not trust the milk or juice supply there either. I asked him why and he said it would make us sick. When the food came, my plate looked okay. Eggs looked good, but there was no toast. There was a very thin-looking pancake but no syrup. Both my brother and my mom's plate looked the same, but my dad's plates looked different. He had ordered "Huevos Rancheros," the eggs looked orange like someone had mixed some sauce in them. My dad told my mom to take a taste. She did and it took her breath away. I stuck to my eggs and Coke and pushed the pancake-looking thing away.

We loaded back in the car, and my dad said we would soon be home. I was so excited. I could not wait to see my house crawl into my bed in my bedroom. I could not wait to see my grandparents. I fell asleep dreaming about it.

Aftermath of 1976 Guatemalan Earthquake

February 4, 1976, Guatemala was rocked by a 7.5 magnitude earthquake. At least 23,000 people lost their lives and a million were left homeless. The area was rocked by aftershocks for almost a month after the original earthquake. Outlying villages and towns from Guatemala City were completely destroyed.

Chapter 8: Home?

Sometime during the second week of February 1976, we finally arrived "home." I had been in and out of sleep most of the day. We pulled up at this two-story duplex late at night. I did not recognize the building. As I awoke, I asked where we were. My dad responded, "At Tia (aunt) Sara's house." *What?! No! Not another aunt.* The last time we went to visit one of his aunts, there was a fire, and then the Earth shook – all in all, not your most pleasant experience. It was memorable, but definitely not pleasant.

I kept asking him, "Are we home?" and he said, "Yes." I assumed what he meant by the home was that we were in Miami, and this was an aunt I had not met. I thought we were stopping there to spend the night because it was really late and dad was too tired to keep on driving. As we exited the vehicle, the scene was all too familiar. We got out of the car, and as we approached the house, I saw there was a woman I had never met in my life who was overjoyed to see us and have us in her home. Up to that moment, it was an instant replay of El Salvador except with a different cast.

As we entered the house, I went into explore mode. I quickly stopped when I noticed pictures of me throughout this woman's house. I had never seen or heard of her, yet she had pictures of my brother and me in her house. I quickly turned around and stood behind my father, who was now seated in this lady's living room. Within a few minutes, my father introduced me to her as "Tia Sara," my father's aunt. She held her arms out and said, "ven aqui Gatica" (in English, it translates as 'come here, my little cat'). This strange woman was calling me a cat? She very quickly explained to me from the very first pictures she saw of me; she named me "Gatica" because of my green eyes.

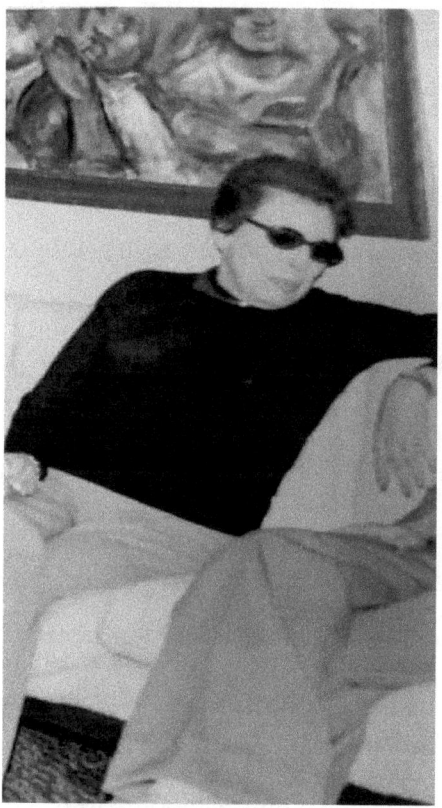

Sara Iglesias

Tia Sara did not live alone. She lived with Tia Elia. We were so tired that within an hour of arriving, we all went to bed. The next morning when I woke up, the adults were already awake and visiting over breakfast. I got out of bed and began exploring. It was not a very big house at all. It was a three-bedroom home with one bathroom. Sara and Elia lived in the upstairs unit of this duplex. As I wandered through, I came to the front window of the living room. While gazing out the window, I could see palm trees swaying in the wind and Spanish-style homes, and yet I did not recognize anything.

After breakfast, we walked out the front door and down the stairs. I was now able to take a good look at Sara's house. It was a white plaster building with a red tile roof. As my parents and Sara came down the stairs, they headed to the pink house with the red tile roof next door. It, too, was a duplex. I was called over. As the door opened, there was a man and his wife, Andy, and Vivian, but most important was their little girl. She was every bit of a two-year-old. As the adults visited, it became very clear to me they were a Cuban family, and so was the other family that shared their duplex. Yes, we were home as far as I was concerned.

The little girl's name was Lizette. She was petite with dark eyes framed by her porcelain white skin. She looked like a beautiful Spanish doll had come to life. From the day we met, she became the little sister I never had. As the day went on, I played with Lizette and my brother. I met her aunt, uncle, and cousin that lived in the unit next door. Her cousin, a little boy, was one year younger than I. We spent the entire day playing, and I quickly forgot about going home. As it became dark, it was time to go home, so I thought.

I asked my dad about when were we to go home, and he replied, "We are home." I told him, "No, this is not my house. My house is yellow with a red tile roof where my bed is." I told him I wanted to see my grandparents and I wanted him to take me to their house. That's when it finally occurred to him that I believed we were in Miami.

As we went into Sara's house, he came in to talk to me and told me we were not in Miami. He told me we were in someplace called Los Angeles. This was our new home, that we were not going to live in Miami and that I wouldn't see my grandparents for a while. He told me that Sara was our family and we would find a place to live nearby. I was devastated. The entire time I was in the car, I dreamt of going home to my house, seeing my family, seeing the palm trees, and feeling the warm tropical air. Going to a place called Los Angeles was definitely not in my plans.

It was not long before we had our own apartment. In fact, we would move into two different apartments within a few months of arriving in Los Angeles, and eventually, life settled into something more normal. Again, normal for my family, not normal for the public at large. My father was gone again for days or weeks at a time working in Central

America; the Sandinista issue. I was attending a Catholic School on Melrose and Vine Street in Hollywood, and my brother was placed in a preschool. This new place also brought other changes than simply the location; my mother began working. So, I lost my home and my mom in a place called Los Angeles.

Christ the King Elementary School

We lived in the Melrose apartment for several years. On Fridays, we normally spent the night at Tia Sara's house. She would always bake something wonderful and watch T.V. with me as long as I watched her and Elia's favorite show, "Dallas." This new life brought a new cast of characters, specifically my father's new business "associates." There was one that was a constant for some time; I only knew him by his nickname, Heuvon.

Heuvon was a bit on the portly side but a nice man. He had a family: a wife and two children, a boy, and a girl. I don't remember their names as we didn't spend much time with his family. In fact, the only time we spent with him and his family was a camping trip we took together. It was the very first time I had ever gone camping. It was also the very first and the very last time my father went camping with us. After this trip, my father always made the comment that he has to camp out a lot during the course of his business, so the last thing he wants to do in his private time is to go camping unless it involves a hotel.

During my father's absence, it was not uncommon to have Heuvon stop by to check on us. We would spend a lot of time with Tia Sara and with Lizette's family. My father and Andy became very close. Andy was very well aware of my father's profession. Vivian, Andy, and Lee (as we called Lizette) became our extended family. It made it easier for my mom, my brother, and me while dad was gone to have some sense of family to spend time with.

Lee's family and mine were inseparable. We vacationed together and made several trips into Mexico, mostly to Tijuana and once to Ensenada. This was during the mid to late 1970s – the era of gas lines, inflation, and Jimmy Carter. It was a very different life than the life I once had in Miami.

Chapter 9: Clear And Present Danger

I was in fourth grade in 1977 when my life began to change again. My father was gone much more during this particular school year. Tia Sara became very ill. She was constantly coming and going from Cedar Sinai Medical Center during this year. It was extremely difficult for my mother to deal with Sara's condition and my father's absence.

Dad was working from Mexico as he went in and out of Nicaragua in the fight against the (Castro) communist-backed Sandinista rebels while we were in Los Angles trying to live a somewhat normal life. Any form of normality went out the window one cold dark evening.

I remember it was a school night, and I had just completed my homework. From that point, it was your average evening. We ate dinner, took our showers, and watched T.V. until it was time to go to bed. A few times during the week, my dad would call and check in with us. I don't remember if this was one of those nights.

As I went to bed, I remember my mother was sitting in the living room on the phone. Bedtime for us was nine o'clock. It had to be past midnight when I woke up to noises and voices. My brother was still sleeping and in bed. I could hear my mother crying. I peeked out of the bedroom and looked toward her room, only to find she was not there. I looked to the living room.

I could see and hear Mom. I could also hear a man's voice. I looked around, and I saw him; it was Huevon. He was holding my mother by the arm, pointing a gun at her. The sight of the gun pointed at my mother caused me to freeze right in that spot. At first, I could not make out what they were saying because she kept on crying.

Finally, I understood. He slowly but in an aggressive tone kept asking her, "Where is he? You know where he is? Tell me now." She told him time and again that she did not know. This went on for a few minutes. Then it changed from "where is he" to "where are your children?" She told him we were in bed sleeping.

He turned and looked toward our bedroom. My mom began to say, "No, No." I panicked. I looked around for a way to get out. There was a window, but it would make too much noise, and I would have to wake my brother first before we could get out. I moved away from the door so he could not see that I was awake.

Huevon began again, "Where is he? You need to tell me. I would hate to have to hurt your children. I will kill your children. Where is he?" My mother lost her mind; she hysterically pleaded, "I don't know! Please don't do anything to the kids! I don't know!" This scene repeated itself a few times. Finally, he stopped. He told her she better find out where he was because her children's lives depended on it and that he told her he would be back. I then heard a door close. I quickly looked out to the living room and saw my mom there, crying and frozen in one place. I ran back to my bed and pulled the sheets over my head.

I did not understand why would Huevon do that. He was my dad's friend. He would check on us when dad was gone. Why would he want to hurt us? I was dazed and confused. It seemed like I was laying there for hours, but it was actually minutes. My mother bolted through our bedroom door, turned our bedroom light on, and told us to get up. My brother was still half asleep as I got up. She then told us to grab a few things. We were leaving; I grabbed a few things too. We walked out the back door of our apartment to our car, got in, and left. It was dark, and my mother drove. She dared not stop; she was too scared. We were on the freeway headed toward Lizette's new house in Burbank.

I am not sure if mom had called Vivian and told her we were on our way, but we flew through her front door. My brother and I were put to bed. I know the adults were awake for a while talking. I know my mom grabbed a phone and tried to call my father.

Somehow, someway, my father was informed of the night's event. Within days, my father was back, and we all returned home. Nothing was said in my presence. Both my parents were unaware that I had seen what happened that night. Sometime after my father's return, news arrived at our house that Huevon had died. He had been killed in his own home with his own gun during a home invasion. My mother had made a comment about how sad she was for his wife and children. I never made a comment, though it would be a while before my father left again.

I think Dad stayed until he felt my mother was ready to deal with being alone again and then the day came when he had to go. The next crisis was of a family nature. Tia Sara had been admitted to Cedar Sinai Medical Center with a massive stroke. Once again, my brother and I were scooped up in the middle of the night but this time dropped off at our babysitter's house while my mother and Vivian went to the hospital.

Tia Sara died that night. The following morning, we were picked up by my mother and Vivian, and we were taken to Vivian's house. I watched as my mother was speaking with my father and telling him it was his responsibility to be there with his aunt, not running around Central America. She told him she would not be attending the funeral unless he came home. She was very upset.

I knew it was best that I stayed away from her. I knew she was dealing with too much, and I needed to be invisible during that time. My father did come home but not in time to attend Sara's funeral.

The summer of 1978 was the first time my brother and I were sent back to Miami to stay with our maternal grandparents and Maggie. Maggie was my mother's youngest sibling. She was 18 years younger than my mom but only five years older than me. Maggie was more my older sibling than my aunt or my mom's sister.

It was wonderful; I was home. It was a carefree summer. Carefree for us but under the protective eye of my dad's associates and colleagues. I have to give it to them. I didn't even notice them. I was just so happy to be home. My grandparents were ecstatic to have us, but they were keenly aware of the eyes watching over us, them, and anyone else we spent time with.

My brother and I spent that summer hanging out with Maggie, visiting family, and swimming. That summer, I had overheard my grandparents talking about the possibility of us moving back to Miami. That would have been my dream come true.

Unfortunately, my dream did not come true, and my brother and I were placed on a plane back to California. We were happy to see our parents. We had returned one week before school started. For the most part, the school year was uneventful—nothing like the year before. The worst thing that happened was that I broke my leg.

Again, as the summer drew near, my brother and I were told we would be going to Miami for the summer. The two of us lazied through our summer while my parents had a very busy summer. In July, my father was back in Nicaragua. The Sandinistas were gaining momentum and were taking the country one city at a time. It was just a matter of time before the capital of Managua would fall.

My father and his crew were sent in to extract Anastasio Somoza Debayle and his family. Yes, all the while I was enjoying myself in fun-filled Florida, my dad was running operations in Nicaragua. Of course, I was not aware of this while it was happening. I would find out about this a few years later.

In the early morning hours of July 17, 1979, my father and his crew evacuated President Somoza and his entourage to an airfield where five planes were ready and waiting to take them out of the country. My father and his crew were armed with AK-47's. The resignation of President Somoza was publicly done in a peaceful manner, but his trip to the airfield and taxing down the dirt runway was not. It was done under fire.

All five planes touched down at Homestead Airforce Base in South Florida that morning. President Somoza's exile would not last long. Under pressure from the Carter administration, he would leave the protection of the United States for Paraguay. He would be assassinated there in 1980.

My father returned home to my mother within days of the end of that operation. He would again be sent back to deal with issues in Central America, only this time to Mexico. This operation I did become aware of while in Miami on summer vacation. I had overheard my grandmother discussing the fall out of it with my grandfather.

The Mexican government had requested the American government to vacate the small compound they occupied where they launched missions out of. They gave them 24 hours to vacate the premises. The American government gave my father the order to vacate, but also to blow the whole thing sky high. He was not to leave any kind of infrastructure or technology for the Mexican government to use. He did exactly what he was ordered; he blew it sky-high.

As my father crossed the border back into the United States, he was arrested for the explosives that were in the trunk of the car he was driving. My mother received the phone call that my father was sitting in a San Diego Jail. This was not the kind of news your wife really wanted to hear, let alone the charges against my father.

My mother appeared in court the day of his arraignment. My father sat behind the Defendant's table, with no representation, while my mother sat quietly in the courtroom. As the district attorney began his rhetoric, a man came through the courtroom doors and asked to approach the bench. He handed a very large file to the judge. The judge opened the file, took a good long look at my father, and he was released to the objection of the District Attorney. The judge did make my father surrender his passport. It was a scene right out of L.A. Law.

That was the final straw. The reason I had overheard my grandparents discussing the matter was that my mother called and told them she was seeking a legal separation. She also asked them to help her find a place to live in Miami. My grandparents were ecstatic with the thought we would be back home. Unfortunately, that did not happen again.

My mother did get separated from my father, but she chose to stay in Los Angeles. My brother and I were boarded on a plane back to California. This time, when we got home, it was to a small run-down duplex my mother had rented...a home without our father. That upcoming school year was spent splitting our time between parents for four months.

Within four months, my father was back living with us. However, his return came with a certain condition. He was to leave "the company." He agreed. He began cutting his ties, at least that's what it seemed like to my mother. When you work within this type of organization, you are never really out unless you are dead. His current choice was between the company and his family. At that moment in time, he chose his family.

Prior to the predawn hours of July 17, 1979, the Somoza family ruled the Republic of Nicaragua and was an American Ally. The Somoza regime worked side by side in the fight against communism by allowing United States operatives to base their operations in Nicaragua. From the Bay of Pigs to providing Nicaraguan troops to fight in Vietnam, Nicaragua was a loyal ally.

Chapter 10: Mariel Boatlift

Mariel Boat

I remember coming through the door from school one afternoon and hearing my parents talking about Cubans fleeing Cuba. When the evening news came on, we all watched it intently; it was a family affair. I was eleven years old and in sixth grade, and even at that age, seeing those news clips was horrifying. As young as I was, I knew those boats weren't just overloaded; they were dangerously overloaded.

These news clips of overloaded boats leaving the port of Mariel played in our home for weeks. Watching those refugees landing in Key West and the first thing they did was kiss the ground was heart-wrenching. I couldn't help but think if they were kissing the ground because they were in the United States, they landed on solid ground or both. Then my thoughts went to all those who may have drowned on the passage over and how terrible it must be in Cuba if they are willing to risk their lives. All of these thoughts were running through my head.

An overloaded boat of Marielitos in Key West

After a few weeks of witnessing the mass exodus of Cuba and seeing the refugee camps popping up all over Miami on the news, I asked my dad why all of this was happening? I thought Castro said Cuba was a utopia? Why are they leaving? I thought Castro didn't allow people to leave Cuba? I was only in sixth grade, but even then, I knew something was terribly wrong, and I wanted to know why.

After the news ended, my dad began to answer some of those questions. He looked at me and said, "Por que (why)? Por que, they are fucking starving, that's why! Why, because Fidel can't feed them, can't house them, and he has no money to run that country! Castro has plundered and rapped the entire island of its resources and has nothing left to take care of the people. That Bastard took care of himself and his family, but everyone else is fucked, ese hijo de puta (son of a bitch)!" He stormed off into the other room for a minute to compose himself; he was really getting riled up. Once he came down from the ceiling, he came back into the room, sat down in his leather chair, and asked me to sit on the floor in front of him.

"Unfortunately, we all knew this was going to happen. What I mean by 'we' is this country along with others. Castro has been a failure from the day he took power. His vision of government is supposed to: provide homes, food, and education. Fidel's Cuba is supposed to take care of you from your first breath to your last. That takes money! He can't provide mierda (shit)! So, to reduce his costs, he is letting as many people out that he can so his Cuba fantasy can continue."

He took a breath and said, "Me entiendes (You understand me)?" I shook my head, yes. He took a deep breath and continued, "The last time there was a boat lift was a few years after he took power, and about five thousand ($5,000.00) people came over by boat and later by plane. This time, it's going to be in the tens of thousands coming over.

I chirped out, "Isn't that good they are coming here?" He looked at me and said yes for them but for this country, no. "What most Americanos don't understand maybe 1/4 of everyone that is coming here are good people, but the rest of them are going to be bad people."

I looked at him and said, "Ay, Papi, that's not fair." He shook his head and said, "Castro is emptying all his prisons, his casas de los locos (mental asylums), and putting them all on boats to Florida." Castro is cleaning the island of anyone he doesn't want, along with a few people who want to leave. We have already been informed he is handpicking the worst criminals and putting them on boats so they can be released on the Miami population. By putting all of them on the boat, he is getting rid of all his undesirables and sending them here. It's a win-win for him. He no longer has to pay for them, so he saves money, and those undesirables are going to cause major problemas in Florida." He got up and walked into the other room, and I went to my room.

As the weeks went by, you saw the refugee camps popping up all around Miami. The news reported; overcrowding, crime was rampant in the camps and surrounding areas. The news broadcasts showed footage from the camps, and it reminded me of the poverty and squaller I saw on our drive to California from Costa Rica. There were numerous times my father was on the phone discussing the "Marielitos," and I knew from the bits and pieces of the conversation he wasn't talking to my mother on the phone.

The Summer of 1980 was a bit different than the past few ones. Yes, my brother and I went to Florida, but this trip, my grandparents and other family member seemed to be more on edge, and we weren't allowed to wander about. The nightly news there was riddled with reports of the soaring crime rate. My grandparents would drive this home; we had to be careful because Miami had turned into a dangerous place.

There were a few times I overheard my grandparents talking about the Marielitos and how Castro sent the worst of the worst to Florida to wreak havoc on Miami, how Castro hated Miami so much for flourishing as Habana crumbled and deliberately unleashed this on Miami to destroy it. My grandmother turned to my grandfather and sniped at him with her finger. Castro is not the only one to blame, "ese hijo de puta (son of a bitch), Carter was warned months ago he was planning this, and that damn peanut farmer did nothing!" I was a kid. I overheard but really did not understand all the bits and pieces that all changed when the Marielitos discussion became part of my high school history class.

Obviously, as I got older, the pieces of the puzzle of the Mariel Boatlift that my father tried to explain and what I overheard came together. During this educational era in California, Castro was not portrayed as a hero for the downtrodden but portrayed every bit as the villain. It was the Deukmejian era in conservative California, and the history books reflected it. As the discussion developed in class, one of my classmates pointed out to the teacher I was Cuban—a rarity at that time. I thought I was going to kill her for pointing me out. At that time in California, most folks really didn't know how to understand a Cuban, let alone any other Latin/Hispanic person that wasn't Mexican. My classmates turned and looked at me like I was an animal under glass or like some endangered species.

As the teacher began discussing the Mariel Boatlift, he kept looking at me for reassurance and asked me questions. I didn't like being the token Cuban. I told him I couldn't answer his questions I was not part of the boatlift. I was not a "Marielito." I don't recall who shouted it out in class. You say that as you're insulted. I said yes, I was; calling any Cuban a Marielito is no different than calling a Mexican a "Beaner or Wet Back." The teacher realized I was really uncomfortable; he quickly changed his tone and continued with the lesson.

That night I came downstairs to get a glass of water to take up to bed when I found my dad downstairs watching TV. I walked into the kitchen, put the glass down, and decided I was going to talk to him about the discussion in class and the whole boatlift issue. I came out from the kitchen, and somehow, he knew I wanted to talk to him because he looked at me and said, Que pasa (what happened)?

I looked at him and said Que Pasa (what happened)? The Mariel Boatlift is what happened. He looked at me befuddled, like where the hell did this come from. I told him it was the topic in class today. "Ah, okay," he said. I said, "I know when it happened; you explained it to me; it came down to Castro's inability to care for his people, but I also heard bits and pieces at Daddy's and Pina's house." He said to me, "and from those bits and pieces, what have you put together?"

I said, "Well, after twenty (20) years of being in power, the embargo made it very difficult to trade; add to that the population grew, and Cuba's government fell far short of its promise of paradise." Cuba couldn't afford to take care of its population. So, he let them leave to cut his costs. One of the best ways to cut his costs is to get rid of all of those who cannot contribute to his Cuban paradise. Castro emptied his prisons, Insane asylums, and any other undesirable and deported them. He knowingly exported his problems to Florida to release the economic pressure in Cuba.

My father's jaw dropped. He was actually stunned by what I had put together. He said, "Is that it?" I said "No. There was one piece I can't figure out." He said, "What is it?"

"Why Abbey said Carter was to blame? I mean, I know he was the President at the time, but he didn't stick people on those boats. He put his hand up, telling me to stop, and nodded his head."

"Well, Carter was made aware of the situation in Cuba in 1979. The imbalance of population to the capabilities of providing for its population. There wasn't housing; there wasn't food, there was nothing! Cubans on the island were desperate. They commandeered a bus and crashed into the Venezuelan Embassy seeking asylum. Carter was told about the situation, and that piece of shit did nothing. He was warned by numerous agencies and governments what was going to happen, not that he could stop it, but he could be prepared for it. Carter was unqualified to be President of this country, let alone grasp the situation in Cuba and how it would affect the United States. He was busy putting his head in the sand regarding the discontent while trying to normalize relations with Cuba. The peanut farmer got schooled by that bearded sugar cane peddler!

You have to understand when Castro said you could leave starting on this day. Anyone and everyone who had a boat in South Florida took off for the port of Mariel to pick up their family members. It was a reverse flotilla. Yachts, fishing boats, pleasure boats, you name it; if it floated and had a motor, it went. Several of my associates chartered boats. Castro and the rest of the world knew exactly what would happen, everyone but for Jimmy fucking Carter.

Boats arrived and sat in the port of Mariel, waiting for permission from the Cuban officials to pick up those people they came for. Cuban Officials boarded those boats and informed them they would not only take back those they came for but those they put on their boats. If they tried to refuse, they would put another captain on that vessel that would comply.

Cuban Officials boarding private vessels

He said those boats that went to Mariel assumed they would get there, grab their people and turn around and go. They thought they would be home within a week. No! They were there for two or more weeks, waiting their turn to pick up their passengers. When it was their turn, they loaded those they came for. Then the Cuban officials began loading others onto the boat. The boats were over capacity, and captains would tell them to stop, and the Cuban officials didn't listen. They kept loading. Captains did what they could, arguing with Cuban officials to stop loading as they were dangerously overloaded, the boat would sink underway if they continued. The Cuban officials said that was a problem for the United States. The Cuban officials wanted the boats to go down, watch the United States deal with this human tragedy on the world stage, or better yet, when they get to Florida; they destroy Miami and the Escoria (excrement/scum) it houses.

There were several boats that went down after leaving the port; most were not reported here in the United States. Cuba celebrated the loss of those boats and the lives on them. Those who made it went into the refugee camps. There was no organization; criminals were housed with decent people. Once those decent people were picked up by their families, the criminal and insane were all that were left, and they roamed the streets of Miami. It was like a human bomb was sent there to destroy Miami."

Cuban Newspaper, Granma Photo, April 1980

I looked at him and said, a human bomb, really? You sound like Castro. I pushed a button that perhaps I shouldn't have. He gave me a stern look and said, "Look, do you know why Castro hates Miami so much? Before I could answer, he went on. It's because Miami is what Habana should be. Miami is Miami because all of those that made Cuba what it was left him and came here and reinvented themselves. The City of Miami thrived while Habana and the rest of the island went to shit. He knows he can't do there what we have done here, and he hates us for it. He hates us because Miami is the very public face of his failure. By releasing all of those criminals and the locos and sending them to Miami, he wants them to destroy the image of the Cuban's in Miami in front of the entire country and world."

I nodded my head in agreement, grabbed my water, and went up to bed. I knew if I said anything else, this discussion would go on for hours. His disclosure regarding Carter gave me an understanding of what my grandmother had said, and the rest of it helped me put Mariel in perspective as a high school student. I also clearly understood why being called a Marielito was so insulting; Marieltos represented Cubans as criminals/scum and the absolute worst kind of person.

In my high school history class, they never mentioned the previous boatlift, but through my research, I found the previous exodus out of Cuba, and it started with a boat lift just like my dad had told me. On September 28, 1965, Castro announced the port Camarioca would be open for those Cubans wishing to leave Cuba and go to the United States could do so. The nearest city to the Port of Camaraioca was Cardenas, my father's hometown.

From the day the rebels took power and implemented their socialist paradise agenda, Cubans were fleeing the island by whatever means necessary. It only got worse when

Cuba declared it was a communist country in 1961. Cubans began taking the hazardous journey across the Florida Straights by boat or any makeshift raft. This was an embarrassment for Castro and the Cuban Government. He declared Cuba a tropical utopia, yet Cubans kept fleeing. At the same time, he came to the realization the country could not sustain itself even with the help of the Soviet Union. The only way to keep the masses believing the revolution was thriving was to control the population. All those that wanted leave would reduce his costs. His decision was a simple economic mathematical equation.

The flood gates were opened, and in came the boats to collect their people. Thousands were at the port, but only three (3) to five (5) thousand Cubans left in this way. They were assisted at sea by the U.S. Coast Guard once they left Cuban waters. In an effort to end the dangerous sea exodus, the United States and Cuba negotiated a safer passage for those wanting to flee the island nation, so began the "Freedom Flights." The flights would continue until 1971.

The airlift ended, but the poverty continued. An economic downturn and a crackdown on dissidents by Cuba's government led to unrest. Cubans fled by sea in boats and makeshift rafts. The steady stream of these rafters (balseros) was a black eye for Fidel. In the late seventies,

Cubans began seeking asylum through embassies; Argentina and Venezuela,

The growing discontent of the Cuban populous posed a serious problem for the Cuban government. Castro recognized it was the same discontent that led them into the revolution. In contradiction to his revolution, this time, it wasn't due to the disproportionate haves to the have nots, but it now was an entire island of have nots—an extremely dangerous situation for any government.

Héctor Sanyustiz Miami Herald Photo

April 1, 1980, a bus driven by Héctor Sanyustiz and a half dozen Cubans desperate to flee the island drove through the gates and breached the Peruvian Embassy. Cuban guards at the embassy fired, wounding the driver, and accidentally killing one of their own police by "friendly fire." The

Cubans requested asylum. Castro ordered the Peruvian embassy to hand over those Cuban nationals to his government. The Peruvian embassy defied Castro's order. They helped and protected those asylum seekers.

Peruvian Embassy in Cuba, April 1980

In retaliation to their refusal of the dictator's order, Castro removed the Cuban guard from the embassy. Over the following next three days, the Cuban asylum seekers went from a handful to 10,856 at the Peruvian embassy. It was a cross-section of Cuban society. Peruvian diplomats held their ground, and refused to turn over the asylees, and held Fidel Castro responsible for the crisis, citing that the Cuban dictator had removed the guards from around the embassy, in violation of international law. The Peruvian government also rejected all requests made by Castro to allow the Cuban military to invade the embassy and remove the asylum seekers forcibly.

Acts of repudiation (actos de repudio) is a term Cuban authorities use to refer to acts of violence and/or humiliation towards critics of the government

Castro's self-created crisis was on full display on the world stage. Instead of diplomacy, he chose to incite those still loyal to his revolution to insult and attack those Cubans looking to leave the country (acts of repudiation (actos de repudio)). Fidel went as far as taking children and youth out of school to take part in acts of repudiation. This was the first time that acts of repudiation were seen when Cubans who simply wanted to leave the country were brutally assaulted, and forty lost their lives in lynchings.

Mariel marked the first-time communist/socialist Cuba turned against itself. The government staged riots called actos de repudio – street rallies in which neighbors turned against neighbors, harassing and tormenting those who wanted to leave the country. The victims were often pelted with rocks, tomatoes, eggs and called Escoria (excrement/scum) and gusano (worms). Windows were shattered. Doors were knocked down. Some people were killed, dragged through the streets as trophies to intolerance and hate. Sometimes people trapped inside their homes choose to kill themselves rather than face their tormentors. Granma, the Communist Party's daily paper, compiled a list of 100 insults to scream at those who wanted to leave. Meanwhile, Fidel Castro prepared to associate these asylum refugees with the worst of the worst; criminals and the insane.

Cuba's Newspaper, Granma April 1980; Demonstrations in Cuba expressing disdain for marielitos and support for the government

Castro had to face the cost of his failed policies. He had to flip the narrative from a failure to a winner. A trick he had mastered. He hit the airwaves making claims as to the conditions in Cuba were due to those who did not believe in the revolution, they didn't contribute to the revolution, and the country would flourish with the exodus of those wanting to leave for the "Yankee Paradise." The island would be cleansed of undesirables. He announced the port of Mariel open, and so began the steady stream of refugees out of Mariel.

Most who fled were members of Cuban exile families already living in the United States. They boarded boats brought by or chartered by relatives to make the crossing to Florida. Cuban officials forcefully boarded other Cuban dissidents on those boats without the consent of or consideration of others. Castro was cleansing the island of those he found undesirable.

Castro didn't hurriedly empty his prisons and asylums, as many have stated. Instead, he took a very steady and methodical approach; Castro scoured prison records brought to him by Jose Abrahantes, the minster of the interior at the time, and lists of prisoners. He hand-selected those that would go; 'Yes 'was for murderers, rapists, pedophiles, and dangerous criminals; 'no 'was for those who had attacked the revolution – political prisoners." Dissidents and political dissidents remained incarcerated. A number of the criminal and psychopathic Marielitos put on the boats to Florida went on to commit heinous crimes — including mass murder, rape, and arson and are incarcerated in United States prisons. Fidel has often denied taking this action, but history has proven his denials to be lies.

Castro also took this opportunity to expunge the island of its homosexual community. From the date Batista government crumbled, the Cuban Government and Castro took on a homophobic stand against the Homosexual community in Cuba. They were fired, imprisoned, tortured, killed, or sent to "re-education camps." All of which costs the government money. He took the Mariel as an opportunity to remove the homosexuals from his island. They were rounded up and sent to the port of Mariel.

Pier B of the Truman Annex during the boatlift

Refugees arriving in Key West, 1980

Trumbo Point Key West, Cuban refugee processing area – Mariel Boatlift

Most Cubans made landfall in Key West. They would be processed in Naval Airbase in Key West, Trumbo Point. The Airbase was converted into a processing center. The refugees would be processed then boarded onto planes and buses to other locations, primarily Miami. Once in Miami, those refugees that had family there, their ordeal ended, but those who did not would be sent to the makeshift refugee camps that were popping up in Miami.

Chapter 11: Mr. Mom

As I have stated, I was far from being the girl next door. However, that would quickly change in junior high. The summer before I began junior high, my family moved from Hollywood to the "burbs." We moved in an area called West Covina in The San Gabriel Valley.

We moved into a townhouse. It was the first house we had lived in since we left Miami, where my brother and I had our own rooms. Along with this move came the move from private school to public school. The biggest change was my dad. He was home all the time. I mean, come on, finding a job after working for "the company" was not easy. How many private-sector jobs need his particular skill set? Could you just see that classified ad:

"A new company needs team players to join its growing management team. The candidate must have the following qualifications:

- Espionage
- Familiarity with explosives
- Mercenary experience is a big plus (bonus pay).

Yep, the newspaper was filled with them. Though he was a naval engineer, imagine the interview and the prospective employer trying to evaluate his skill set: "So, when you blew someone away, on a scale of one to ten, would you say you did that efficiently or could you have found a more efficient way to conduct your job that would save the company money?" Or, about references, "Hello, Mr. U.S. Official, Mr. so-and-so worked under your direct command and indirectly running operations that the government never acknowledged publicly, but I need you to rate Mr. so-and-so's performance." Sure, it happens every day.

Perhaps it was a blessing in disguise for him. You see, it was not soon after we moved that my mother found out she was pregnant. Not only was she caught off guard, but we all were too. I mean, come on, I was already 13, and my brother was 11. A baby? Needless to say, we all were expected to pitch in with this baby, and Dad was a key member of the baby project.

Crystina and Leanne

In May of 1981, my sister was born. She was perfect in every way and became dad's full-time job. He went from being James Bond to Mr. Mom in a jiffy. I'm sure he never imagined this role change. He did the grocery shopping, cooked us meals, ran my brother and me to our swim practices, and took care of the baby. It was during that time my dad realized how much he missed out with my brother and me growing up – how much he sacrificed and almost lost. He made a few comments about it to me during my sister's first year.

Time and again, when I came home from school, I would find my father on the phone talking to somebody. I never knew who exactly was on the other line, but I knew it was business—the type of business he wasn't supposed to be conducting. I stayed quiet about it.

One afternoon, I came home from school early due to a minimum day schedule. My father must have forgotten. When I approached the house, I noticed a man in a suit at the door just standing there. As I approached the door, my father saw me and called to the man and told him to let me in. I walked into the house and found my dad speaking with another man in a suit. I picked my sister up and walked through the living room, up the stairs to my room.

During those brief moments, I overheard the man tell my father, "It is just the operation he had been waiting for." The men weren't there long after I got home. As soon as they left, my father came to my room and asked me to come downstairs to talk to him. My sister was asleep, and I had set her in her crib. I went downstairs as I was asked. My father motioned for me to have a seat on the couch.

Dad started out by asking me not to say a word to my mother as to what I saw and heard that afternoon. I promised I would not tell her. He also told me he turned down their offer. However, he would help by consulting via telephone in any way. I didn't understand why he was telling me this. He had never told me anything before about what he did; why now?

Well, quite frankly, I was old enough to understand. My father had no idea how much I already knew and understood, but I am sure he suspected. This would be the first of many unconventional father-daughter conversations we would have during my teenage years. I mean, most fathers have conversations with their daughters about boys, growing up, peer pressure, and sex. My father's conversations were to fill me in on his life experiences. It was during this conversation that I found out why we actually moved to Costa Rica, about his work in Nicaragua and the extraction of Somoza, and finally, his brief stint as a guest of the San Diego County Jail.

This first conversation filled in a whole lot of holes about things I only knew portions of. It was explained to me that at the first sign of danger, all he had to do was make a phone call, and we would be extracted and taken somewhere safe to start over. This conversation made me that much more aware of how dangerous it really had been and still was for us because there really were people out there looking for him. That conversation fueled and manifested itself into repetitive nightmares of my family being in constant danger in the wake of my father's mercenary work. My nightmares would continue every night until my second year of marriage.

As months passed during the first part of my eighth-grade year, it wasn't uncommon for me to get home and find my father on the phone talking to someone. There came a day that the phone rang at our house and my father and I picked up the phone at the same time. I was upstairs, and he was downstairs. Remember, I was very curious by nature, and I had mastered the art of eavesdropping. It was my uncle, my mother's brother.

My uncle had been caught as a mule. Okay, a quick definition of the term "mule" in this context; someone transporting drugs from one point to another. In his case, the drug he was caught with was cocaine. My uncle was calling my dad to get him out of the mess he was in. My father instructed him to keep his mouth shut and to sit tight, that he had to make some phone calls. He was very specific; if he was going to help my uncle, my uncle had to follow his instructions to the letter or he would not help him. My uncle agreed and the call ended. It wasn't five seconds later when I heard my name being called.

I went down the stairs, and there he was waiting for me. All my father said was, "I know you were on the phone." As far as you are concerned, that phone call never happened, and he would choose the time and place to let my mother know about her brother's situation. He handed me the baby, and I watched my father as he made phone call after phone call calling in favors. Within the hour, my father was on the phone with my grandfather and informed him the situation had been handled and not to worry.

I wasn't there when he told my mother, but I do remember him telling me the outcome. Bottom line, my uncle had to sing like a canary, agree to turn over the names of the higher-ups, and the government would give him a new identity. I was in awe of him. All of that was handled in an hour's worth of phone calls.

It was during my eighth-grade year that I was allowed to take babysitting jobs. There was one condition though; I could only babysit for people my parents knew. That's when life with the "Argentinos" began. There was an Argentine family we became friends with through Lizette's family, who had a daughter five years younger than me and an even younger brother. Their family was in the same situation we were in. Most, if not all, of our families were far away from their "home." So, we became each other's family.

Yes, it was a bit odd. You see, most Cubans aren't fond of "Argentinos" because of their most famous export: "Che Guevera," or better known as "El Che." He was Castro's right-hand man and helped Castro take over Cuba. It has been said that without "Che," Castro would have been just another rebel in the mountains that would have ended up in Batista's prisons. Something Castro recognized and would later make sure "El Che" would not pose a threat to him by sending him to Bolivia to spread the revolution. In actuality, Castro purposely sent "Che" away so he could be killed and made a martyr for the revolution. I remember my father telling me he had only a few regrets, one of them; He was not present when "El Che" was killed, and he was not present when Fidel received the box with "El Che's" hands.

These Argentinos were the exception to the rule. They were family and have remained as such to this day. I regularly babysat their kids and became very close with their daughter Lesley. We would become like sisters, much like my sister and I, and Lizette and I. My father was Mr. Mom, but he was also still working to some extent. It was during my eighth-grade that my father began giving me a type of history lesson. This was the year I began to question everything that was taught to me about modern history. These are the lessons I still use today and pass on to my children.

Ernesto Guevera Lynch (Che Guevera); Che is an oxymoron, a medical doctor who preferred to take lives than to save them. It has been said without "Che," there would have been no Cuban Revolution. Without Che, Fidel would have gone down in history as a failed revolutionist who spent the remainder of his life rotting away in jail if not executed. Unfortunately for the island nation, Fidel had Che, and with both of them working together, successfully took control of Cuba.

Shortly after rising to power, "Che" was put in charge of La Cabana. It is said 55 executions occurred as a direct order of Che and several hundred others at this fortress. He justified the revolution as a Human Rights movement. He executed hundreds of people without due process/trial. Anyone who did not agree with the revolutionary regime found themselves at the wall for execution.

Che was a victim of his own success. Many in the regime noted Che's popularity with the masses none more than Fidel. Fidel was not blind to Che's popularity and the threat it posed to him. He played on Che's revolutionary loyalty by charging him with the spreading of the revolution. The "Second Revolution" was an immense failure known as

Angola (Congo). In his memoir, Che admitted defeat and stated, "We can't liberate by ourselves a country that does not want to fight." Returning to Cuba was an impossibility as a failure after Castro had read his farewell letter to the nation, a letter only to be read in the event of Che's death. Che chose to wander in Dar es Salaam and Prague for six months with Cuban intelligence's false identity papers. He would test those false documents throughout western Europe and then secretly travel to Cuba to meet with Castro and see his family before accepting his next revolutionary local, Bolivia.

Castro knew that by sending Che to Bolivia, he was sending him to his certain death. For Castro, it was an easy trade eliminating the only threat to his power by making him a martyr to the cause; a dead man cannot rule. On October 9, 1967, Che came to the end of his rope. He was captured on October 8, 1967, at his Yuro Ravine encampment in Bolivia by Bolivian Special Forces with the assistance of CIA Operatives. On October 9, 1967, Bolivian President Rene Barrientos ordered the execution of Che. Che was to receive the news of his execution by CIA operative Felix Rodriguez.

The Capture of Che Guevera; from left to right Felix Rodriguez and Che Guevera.

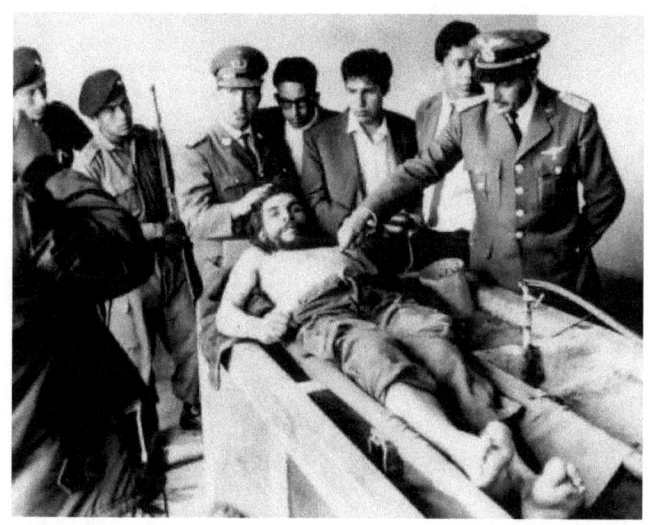

Execution proceedings of Che Guevara, New Yorker Magazine

The United States did not want Che's execution; on the contrary, they wanted Che extradited to Panama for questioning. The governing authority was Bolivia, and they had the final say on the matter. Che was executed, his hands severed from his body for confirmation of his identity via fingerprints in his home country of Argentina, and later delivered to Fidel.

It has been reported during the hours before his death that Che declared Fidel betrayed him. He was right; he was betrayed by the revolution for the revolution. His death made him a martyr and secured Fidel's unchallenged grip on Cuba.

Chapter 12: The Aranzazu

High school is like spending four years on a rollercoaster; everybody goes through it. I was no different except for the added issue of how to answer the inevitable question: "What do your parents do for a living?" Mom was easy; a bookkeeper. Dad? I did not know what to say. Hmmm, "he's like James Bond, but a Ricky Ricardo version. My only other alternative was to go with the Mr. Mom title. Either way, as a high school student, I would sound like some nut or some loser, but so goes the life of a typical teenager. I opted to go for the Mr. Mom route. To be honest, it very rarely came up, which made my life much easier.

My freshman year, 1982, was pretty normal aside from your normal teenage drama; it was great. Now that following summer…that is a totally different story. Unlike the summers before, I had no trip to Miami coming. My mother, brother, and baby sister were going, but I, being the oldest child, had to stay home and become responsible. So is the curse of the eldest child; always used to set an example for the younger siblings. Never mind that nine times out of ten, when it came turn for the younger siblings to follow the example, they are never made to, but that is a different topic for another time. So, it was going to be just my dad and me for a few weeks that summer. What a summer it was!

My father had planned a gathering at our place for the 4th of July. The Argentinos and Lizette's family were coming over. There was going to be a barbecue, swimming at the pool, and fireworks. The "fireworks" that would start off in the early afternoon were not the traditional kind, though.

Everyone arrived, and the party began. My father was in the front patio starting the barbecue when some man began to scale the wall between our balcony and the neighbor's balcony.

My father told the guy to get down, and the guy blew my dad off while brandishing a gun. My father immediately called the police. In less than three minutes, our townhouse was surrounded by the police and SWAT. I, as usual, was oblivious. I was in my room with Lesley and Lizette, unaware of what was going on. In less than sixty seconds, everyone became very aware.

Suddenly a policeman came through my balcony window and ordered us face down on the ground. I don't think anybody had seen three girls hit the floor faster. Simultaneously, the same scene was going on downstairs, except everyone eating dirt downstairs was adults. Once the police finished storming the place, we were all cleared to get back up and resume our "holiday" festivities. The cops were also in the townhouse next door. Unfortunately, our neighbors were gone for the weekend, and although the cops did not catch the man in their home, they did score something else; their marijuana plants.

As I said, the afternoon fireworks started the festivities off with a bang. At the end of the day, everyone went home with a very memorable fourth, and I was left with an inebriated dad. As we both began to clean up, my dad began talking to me about the trip he and mom took to Spain when I was little. You know the one when I set all the bells and whistles off in our house in the middle of the night. The conversation began with a very simple comment. He said this was not the first time he tried to leave the company; he tried to get reassigned, and that's what the trip to Spain was all about. I turned around and looked at him. He clearly had my undivided attention.

Dad sat down and poured his guts out to me. Apparently, he was offered a position within the DEA, and he would be based out of Spain. The purpose of the trip was for training, house hunting, and to get me enrolled in school. He passed his training, they found a house and had me enrolled in school. He stopped and looked at me. I remember thinking we could have moved to Spain. Wow, that would have been so cool. I looked at Dad and asked him about what had happened and why didn't we move to Spain. He went on to tell me that when the Spanish government found out "he" was in the country and that "he" would possibly be residing in their country, they very quickly notified him and the DEA that they did not want him in the country, and very politely (his words) asked him to leave.

Christ, all I could think was "ejected!" How does someone get ejected from a foreign country?! Come on, I knew why he was ejected from the United States, but Spain…well, I was no longer a little girl, and I had a mouth for questions. Before I knew it, the following words came rolling out of it: "How on Earth does someone get thrown out of Spain before you even get to move there?" His response was short and to the point. "Some innocent men died because of faulty information; it happened before you were born."

"This operation had us attacking facilities off the North Coast of Cuba, but when we got to the landing point, we found it lit up like a fucking Christmas tree (again, his words). We had to abort. Instead, we intercepted a vessel, and innocent men died. We had bad intelligence. We had our orders," he said in a very sobering tone.

"There were two swift boats, the Monty and the Gitana, and the mother ship, the Santa Maria. I was the naval engineer of record for the operations, and I was on the Santa Maria. All under the cover as the Dominican Navy, all of our identification was also Dominican Navy. We were in Bahamian waters; it was a foggy night. As all three of our vessels cut through the fog, the lead vessel captained by Santiago Alvarez made out the name on the boat as "Sierra." They identified the vessel as the "Sierra Maestra," the flagship of the Cuban Merchant Marine bound for Cuba and loaded with weapons. They called in for permission for fire.

"The call went out to Felix Rodriguez for permission to open fire. Felix could not get a hold of Manuel Airtime but gave us permission as long as the ship was the Sierra Maestra. The authorization was passed along to the two lead boats. They opened fire. By the time Santa Maria approached the vessel, and I saw the name "Sierra Aranzazu," I realized the intelligence was bad, and they had opened fire on the wrong boat.

"I boarded the vessel and found the captain and some crew had been shot. I had a mess on my hands. I made the decision to round up the surviving crewman of the vessel and place them in the lifeboat, and sent them adrift, knowing they would be rescued in a short period of time by a passing vessel. I inspected the cargo and found ham and other commodities. This went from a simple operation to an international incident all on my watch.

"There was no easy way out of this situation. After the boat had been cleared of its crew, I was ordered to scuttle the vessel. The boat was burned. The few crew members that survived identified me to the Spanish government. When your mother and I went to Spain, the Spanish government became aware of my presence as well as the possibility of my new position. The Spanish government quickly had the offer rescinded and asked that I leave the country."

I sat there staring at him. He just told me men were killed over Spanish Ham. Due to that "incident," he was turned down for the position based in Spain. I could not blame Spain for not wanting my father in their country after such a botched operation that caused the lives of innocent men.

I remember making a comment, "Spanish Ham? You guys burned a boat and killed people, and the boat didn't have any weapons so the Sierra Maestra made it to Cuba?" Dad looked at me and said the Sierra Maestra made it to its port the week before.

That night I lay in bed thinking about my day's events. I became one with my bedroom carpet during the afternoon raid, and I found out the truth about my parents' trip to Spain. I think I could have done that without the eating of the carpet part. It would be one of the most memorable Fourth of July's of my life.

The internet age brought me more information. I searched for the Sierra Maestra and the Sierra Aranzazu. I found the actual date in September that my father's operation did go way wrong. It was September 14, 1964, four years before my birth.

Apparently, the main base for the operations, those calling the shots that night, were in Nicaragua, Monkey Point. The accounts of the operation made it apparent that permission to fire upon the vessel was made by the decision-maker, a man named Felix Rodriguez. He gave the go-ahead, only if the lead ship was certain that it was the Sierra Maestra. Mr. Rodriguez's decision was based on intelligence given to him by the lead boat captain. That, coupled with radio silence (he made several attempts to contact his superior 'Manuel Airtime') from the contacts in the US Government, sealed the fate of the Spanish Merchant Ship.

Cuba blamed the United States for the attack on an unarmed Spanish Merchant Ship. To be exact, Castro claimed it was a Cuban Exiles group backed by the CIA, while Spain was looking to the United States for answers as to how such an attack could happen in the United States-controlled territory, patrolled by its Navy. The United States contended the attackers did not come from US territory but floated the possibility of raider attacks perpetrated by Renegade Cuban Exile groups out of Central America. I found it pretty ironic that Castro and the United States actually agreed on something. The United States omitted the part of its story that they were providing the information and backing the Renegade Cuban Exile Group.

My father was right. The Sierra Maestra had made port in China a week or so earlier. The vessel had cleared the Panama Canal and was headed to China at the time of the attack on the Sierra Aranzazu. The captain and another crew member died, the survivors were picked up by passing Dutch Vessel and ferried to Cuba. The operation must have been an embarrassment to the United States.

Over the years, I would hear the story, and a little bit more information would come out. In interviewing my mother, she told me on this operation, there was a photographer, Jim Nickless, onboard the mother ship, Santa Maria, who photographed the mission. Those photographs were delivered to her for safekeeping. The Cuban government was aware she had the photographs and wanted to publish them in their newspaper, "The Granma" to show the world the United States was behind the attack.

My mother was followed shortly after receiving the photographs, and a car bomb went off close to my parents' apartment. As you can imagine, my father, along with the rest of the crew from this operation, were detained for questioning, leaving her alone with this situation. She called my grandfather (yes, he too, in a way, was involved with the company but more on that in later chapters), and my grandfather made the decision to turn the photographs to the

FBI. The photographs were delivered to Jimmy Hayes of the FBI.

The Sierra Aranzazu was built by Santander Corcho shipyards and was the sister ship of the Sierra Maestra, the Cuban Merchant Marine Vessel. On that fateful night, due to weather, the Sierra Aranzazu was mistaken for Cuba's Sierra Maestra. The permission to open fire on the ship was given based on mistaken identity. Ultimately the "autonomous" group named responsible for this tragic event was; El Movimiento de Recuperacion Revolucionaire (MRR), whose founder was Manuel Airtime. Felix Rodriguez was among its prominent members, along with my father. It was Felix who gave permission with the caveat of the verification of the vessel as the Sierra Maestra.

As the Mother ship, Santa Maria, approached through the fog, my father made out the name and realized the error made by the patrol boat's captain. It was too late the Sierra Aranzazu had taken several hard blows, severely damaging the ship. As he boarded the vessel, he found the captain and two crew members dead. He verified the cargo and radioed the situation to base, Felix. He was ordered to scuttle the ship; he set her aflame.

Dad made the decision to have the surviving crew members of the Sierra Aranzazu lowered in a life raft and set adrift. A Dutch vessel would come across the lifeboat with the crew members. The crew members were ferried to Cuba.

Sierra Aranzazu Lifeboat with surviving crew, September 14, 1964

The Cuban authorities towed the still burning hull of the ship into Antilla, the Oriente Provence of Cuba.

The burned vessel Sierra Aranzazu was towed into the port of Mariel

Chapter 13: JFK

Who hasn't heard of "JFK," "Dealey Plaza," and "Lee Harvey Oswald?" How about the date November 22, 1963? Yes, that's the date of the assassination of President John F. Kennedy. During my Junior year in 1985, I was given an assignment. My teacher was going on about how everybody knew exactly where they were when they heard that John F. Kennedy had been assassinated. The assignment was to include interviews with our parents – great, just the kind of assignment I've always wanted!

For the record and for those out there who do not know the lack of love the Cuban exile community has for the Kennedy family, let me inform you; if anyone mentions the Kennedys, you will get a familiar response: "Thank God that bastard is dead." Heaven forbid you refer to them as

America's royal family. Their response will be something like: "John Kennedy was a womanizing bastard, the son of a bootlegger, and owed his political victory to the mob and teamsters." Then there is the most common comment: "A good Kennedy is a dead one."

Having all of this in the back of my mind, I really wasn't looking forward to this assignment. When I got home, I waited for my mom. She would be the first one I would interview. I posed the question to her, "Mami, where were you when you heard JFK had been killed?" She turned, looked at me, and said, "I was at home with the Dobermans." I then asked where Papi was? She said he was in Keys. I dropped him off at Homestead Air Force Base the day before and picked him up the day after in Key Largo. I knew my father's answer was not going to be just a simple one-liner.

I went downstairs, sat across from my dad, and told him I needed to interview him for a school project. I posed the same question, "Where were you when JFK was killed?" His response, "I was at a bar in the Keys all day." I asked him if he remembered what he was doing when he heard the news the president of the United States had been assassinated. He said, "Yes, I raised my glass with the rest of the patrons and toasted his death." To be exact, he said the toast that was given was: "Salud, the fucking bastard is dead!"

I looked at him and said, "Wait a minute, what do you mean the patrons in the bar were toasting his death? How did you find a bar full of JFK haters?" He chuckled and said, "I know you are reading about him in history, but remember, history is just a story, and like all stories, you need to be able to read between the lines. Historical events are always changing to fit the narrative of whoever is in power at the time. Every historical event is never quite as it seems." I gave him a look and wondered, *what does this have to do with my assignment?*

He began by telling me he had been ordered to be at a specific place, el cayo sin Nombre (No Name Key) that day. When he arrived, he recognized most of the people in the bar. Some were operatives he had worked and based with while others were individuals who had some involvement in the "Bay of Pigs" and other operations. I interrupted him and said, "Wait a minute; you mean to tell me you knew John F. Kennedy, the American president, was going to be killed and you did nothing? He said, "First of all, that man was not worthy of that office; he was a fucking bastard. And second, he got what was coming to him. He, his father, and his brother signed his death warrant, and no, I did not know exactly what was going to happen or if it had anything to do with John Fucking Kennedy. I cannot say if anybody in that bar that day knew the specifics, but I realized by the collection of characters that we were in this public place for a purpose: so that we all had credible public alibis."

"Alibis for what?" I asked.

"I did not know until the announcement came over the bar's radio that Kennedy had been shot. At that one single moment, the entire bar was quiet," he said in that instant. "Everyone realized the reason they had been ordered to be there. With that, someone called for a toast. All glasses were raised, and the toast was made. Salud, the fucking bastard is dead! Was I happy he was dead? You bet your fucking ass I was."

I asked him why they lied about it, and more importantly, about how did the American public buy the whole lone gunman story. He looked at me and said, "The American public is fed what it needs to know, just enough to satisfy their outcry but less than the entire truth. The American public could not handle the entire truth of what goes on in the political world both here and abroad. Europeans know more about what goes on here than the average American Citizen," he said. "Everything was very well planned right down to the staging. It made for an easy sell; further, the American population would have never accepted the fact that their own government was in on it or knew anything about the assassination plot."

As I sat there digesting what my father had just told me, I realized I'd have to make up some lame story for where he was. Could you just see it:

Teacher: So Sally, where were your parents on that fateful day?

Sally's response: Well, my parents were at home in shock that the president had been shot. All my mother could do was cry.

Teacher: How about you, Johnny?

Johnny: My dad left work as soon as he heard of it to be with my mom.

Then, of course, they would get to me: Oh yeah, my father was ordered to be at bar all day, and when the announcement came on the radio that JFK had been shot, all the bar-goers lifted their glass to make a toast. "Salud! The fucking bastard is dead!" Yep, that would have gone over like a ton of bricks. A grade of "F" was a certain guarantee.

My father wasn't quite done with his commentary on John F. Kennedy. He continued: "You see, Mr. Kennedy pissed off a lot of people and double-crossed some very powerful people. Good ole Joe Kennedy made a deal with the devil to get his boy elected. He went to bed with the mob, and the mob delivered the teamster's vote. The mob does not do anything out of the kindness of their hearts. You know, Mr. Kennedy's biggest mistake was naming his brother

Bobby as Attorney General. Bobby made it his priority to go after the mob. He went after one mob member with fervor; Marcello. The bastard was going after the very group he owed his brother's job to. That was mistake number one. Mistake number two was going after the CIA and trying to curtail its power. Mistake number three was the Kennedy brothers' double crossing of the Cuban commandos in the "Bay of Pigs" and denying air support at the last minute as the commandos were landing on the beach. Then, of course, there was Fidel; he was pissed off at the Kennedy brothers for the failed attempts on his life. Every step those two brothers took was straight into shit. In some way, shape, or form, most of these groups had their hands in John F. Kennedy's death. Joe Kennedy made a deal with the devil, and his sons tried to double-cross the devil; they simply lost."

I wasn't going to ask about Bobby's death. That would have been another long dissertation. He did make one statement: "There will never be another Kennedy in the White House." I remember responding to him, "There is always Teddy." He looked at me and said he would not dare. I asked why and he said that during his last attempt at running for the presidency, Teddy received a note informing him he would be killed like his brother should he run. Papi looked at me and smiled. He said that a few days after Teddy received that note, he announced he was not going to run due to family responsibility.

We are taught in school not to question historical events and facts, and here I was staring at living proof that JFK was not killed by a lone gunman named Lee Harvey Oswald like our history book said or the Warren Commission found. My father had been given his orders days before the assassination, which means this was a very well-planned assassination of an American president. I had always loved history. Now I would look at historical data in a different way, as a matter of opinion formed by the available factual data and those in power at the time the opinion was written or re-written. I questioned history, news event, and just everything. I question everything. Consequently, I have never, and still do not, swallow what people try to spoon-feed me.

During the early and mid-1960s, South Florida and the Florida Keys was a hot bed for anti-Castro activity. Cuban exiles trained by the CIA for the Bay Pigs invasion and other operations were based in these areas, as well as others. After the Bay of Pigs invasion failed, more commonly known as the Bay of Pigs "betrayal," covert operations continued. In the case of my father, he had been operating out of the Florida Keys.

Operations and training were common in the Marathon-Sombrero Key, Big Pine Key, and No Name Key areas. The close proximity to Cuba along with the multiple canals facilitated operations. All operations were executed with the knowledge and financial backing of the CIA. However, if any operations were discovered and exiles arrested, as is standard practice, the United States would deny any association with the "Renegade Cuban Exile Community."

On November 22, 1963, my father was ordered to be at a bar on No Name Key, known today as No Name Pub. All day long. He was told what he needed to know and nothing more. When he arrived and looked around, the bar contained a who's who of the operative community. He knew the sole purpose of such a gathering was to be seen in a public place for credible alibis. As the day's events unfolded, all in the bar were made aware of their need for the alibis. All in the bar knew the moment the announcement came over the bar radio of the assassination of John F. Kennedy was not a random act, but a well planned covert operation involving collusion on separate levels of different government entities – federal, state, and local, along with the mob and private sector funding.

In 1991, Oliver Stone released the movie *JFK*. It was an acclaimed movie based on the conspiracy of the assassination of John F. Kennedy. Though much of the film was somewhat accurate of what actually transpired in Dealy Plaza that day and the events leading up to that day, it also contained liberties to try to tie ends, to make the puzzle fit, or to make Hollywood magic. My father's comment after seeing the movie was, "Oh, so close but no cigar."

In further discussions with my father, all those present at that bar had worked with government entities, the mob, involved in anti-Castro activities, or did all of the above. Given a highly publicized investigation would be the aftermath of an event, all those present would be suspected of some knowledge and or participation. That could not be allowed to happen due to the multitude of cross-use of all of the assets present that day at No Name Pub by all of the possible suspects.

History will always portray past presidents as "great." It not only portrays Kennedy as a "great" president, even though his presidency was a failure, but also made him a martyr. A martyr, for the American people, much like Che Guevara, is the martyr for Castro's Cuba – both murdered indirectly at the hands of their own country and cause.

Chapter 14: November 24, 1963

All Americans know the date November 22, 1963, but most Americans don't recognize the date November 24, 1963, or don't remember the significance of that date. In the early afternoon hours of November 24, 1963, the very public, televised hit of the "Lone Assassin of JFK," Lee Harvey Oswald, took place in Dallas, Texas. The neat and tidy end to an American dilemma.

Obviously, I was aware of the why and whereabouts of my father on November 22, 1963, which contradicted what I was being taught in my American history class. Well, if my father was the embodiment of that contradiction, then the next logical conclusion was the lone gunman theory I was being taught had to be wrong, right? Well, after I received my JFK assignment back, I gave it to my dad to read.

After my dad read it, he chuckled. I looked at him and said, "Oh yeah, that's really funny. What did you expect me to write? Now I have to listen to the Warren Commission shit show and hold my tongue. I know the Warren Commission report is inaccurate; better stated, it's a mythical fable. They might as well have stated a rainbow-colored unicorn did it not Lee Harvey Oswald; either conclusion is just as believable." He stayed quiet, then I asked him, where were you when Oswald killed?!

He said, "In bed." What? I replied. He repeated; I was in bed with your mom in our apartment watching TV. We were watching Oswald being transferred just like most Americans. To which I responded, "In bed, in the afternoon?" I rolled my eyes and said, at least you were home; this time, you weren't ordered to be somewhere else. So began another unusual father-daughter conversation.

"Your mother and I were watching the TV and watched the whole thing happen. Right after it happened, I knew exactly what happened. Your mother and I just witnessed a hit. I told your mom to get dressed; we were going to her parents' house." I recall telling him "That sounds logical. You see Oswald killed on TV, and you go to my grandparents' house. You guys wanted to be with family; I get it."

He replied, "Something like that."

I recall envisioning him and my mom walking through the door of my grandparents' house and finding an entire Cuban family huddled around the TV set; My grandfather, my grandmother, and my uncle, Maggie was just a baby, so she would have been in a playpen while the rest of them would be listening to news and running their own commentary on the whole assassination of Oswald. My dad noticed my mind went elsewhere and said; "Psst, where did you go?" I told him what I envisioned, and again my father chuckled.

As he explained it to me, what I envisioned was partially correct. My grandparents, just like every other person in the United States, were watching Oswald as he was being transferred to the county jail. Why were they and the rest of America watching? Well, all of the news channels, all three of them, ABC, CBS & NBC, had announced the time and date of the scheduled transfer, and they would have reporters present to televise it live. Newsmen like Walter Concrite, Dan Rather, and Peter Jennings, reported on the impending transfer.

"The whole world knew the time and date. There was no way Oswald was going to be allowed to live and tell his tales. The country could not afford the fallout; there was too much at stake," he said. I rolled my eyes and flippantly said; so, whoever or whatever organizations orchestrated your little trip to the bar the day JFK was assassinated had Oswald off'd? He curtly replied, "Yes."

I knew from the tone in his voice he was not all happy with my flippant attitude and that I should tread lightly. What I should have done and what I did were two totally different things. Common sense would dictate; instead of being an insolent teenager, I should have been the respectful daughter. Unfortunately, like most teenagers, common sense was not my strongest suit; had it been so, I probably would have gotten more answers about that day from him than I did.

Well, I opened my rude little mouth and said, "So you and the entire family just sat around my grandparents' house eating chips, having drinks watching this play out on TV like you watch the Super Bowl." Make no mistake, he picked up on my condescending attitude and tartly replied, "No, your grandmother and I left the moment your mother and I arrived. I have no fucking clue what your grandfather, your mother, and uncle did after we left." I should have left well enough alone because I knew I pissed him off, but I didn't. I couldn't help myself. I pushed the envelope; "what do you mean you left with my grandmother?" I got no response to that question. All I got was a very stern look. You know that look. It's that look you get from a parent that you pushed beyond the line, and if you persisted, you would be grounded for life.

Somehow common sense stepped in and took over. I got up, left the living room, and went to my bedroom. I knew he was not going to tell me anything more, not because he didn't want to but to teach me a lesson. That lesson was to learn how to read those you want information from. It also reaffirmed any child's survival instinct; don't rattle a parent.

Lee Harvey Oswald shot at point blank range by Dallas night club owner Jack Ruby, in the garage of Dallas police headquarters

I never really asked him about it again. Years later, while watching the JFK documentary with my mother, I asked my mother where she was on the day Lee Harvey Oswald was assassinated? She said exactly what my father had said; she was in bed watching TV with him and saw Oswald's death unfold right in front of her. She said it was unbelievable; she could not believe what she had just witnessed on national TV.

I thought about peppering her with questions but remembered the lesson I learned from my dad the last time this topic was broached. Instead, I just let her go. She continued. My father jumped out of bed and immediately began getting dressed. He told her to get dressed; they had to leave immediately to get to her parents' house.

When they arrived at her parents' house, my father and grandmother left, she said. I asked her where did they go? She said, "I have no clue. You didn't ask them when they got back that evening?" She said, "That evening? No, they were gone for about two days. I was stranded at my parents' house with my father, my brother, and Maggie, the baby. Wherever they went your grandfather was very uncomfortable, he was very worried." I said, "So they left together and were gone for days? She said, "No. They did not leave together. They left at the same time in separate cars." She said she later learned my dad went to his base in the keys, and my grandmother went to a safe house in Miami.

I had no idea at the time of my conversation with my dad why my grandmother went anywhere, to begin with, let alone where either of them went on that day. My father never said they were gone for a few days. I assumed they left and returned that evening. I had to learn early on, assuming in this family was a dangerous business.

Having the understanding of my father's whereabouts on November 22, 1963, and why he was there, I knew Lee Harvey Oswald was silenced. I've always wondered if Oswald knew the role he was playing or was he being played? Either way, he had to have known the possibility of the ultimate consequence of the game he was a pawn in. I am sure that in 1963, America Oswald felt safe in the custody of police and with the strong presence of the press.

As a high-profile accused assassin of John F Kennedy, Oswald must have thought, as would have anyone at that time, he would be kept safe for trial. Nobody, not the CIA, FBI, or even the Dallas police, would have done such a public hit. Tying up loose ends in a very public way this time in history in America was the calling card of another organization.

On November 22, 1963, Lee Harvey Oswald was apprehended at the Texas Theater, a movie theater in the neighborhood of Dallas known as Oak Cliff. At the time of his arrested, he was charged with the death of police officer J.D. Tippit. While in the custody of the Dallas police later that day, the charge of the assassination of JFK was added.

This was the first time live TV made the American population witnesses to a murder. Some say it was the birthplace of reality TV or 24-hour news. From November 22, 1963 – November 26, 1963, there was 24-hour news coverage. All three major networks, ABC, CBS, and NBC, suspended all regular programming to cover the assassination and all the pursuant events.

It made a villain out of Lee Harvey Oswald, a vigilante out of his murder, Jack Ruby, and left so many loose ends. Questions and doubts still abound. One thing is for certain someone definitely didn't want Oswald talking to anybody.

Lee Harvey Oswald was born in New Orleans on March 18, 1939. At the time of his birth, he was fatherless; his father died two months prior to his birth. His childhood was unconventional and unpredictable. He lived in Louisiana, Texas, and New York. It is rumored he attended 22 schools. He was a loner who had detached himself from the world around him and immersed himself in a fantasy life of a grandiose perception of himself. He had issues getting along in school, which resulted in truancy and disciplinary actions. By 1956 he had dropped out of school and joined the Marines.

His troubles followed him in the Marines. He was court-martialed twice, the first time for "accidentally" shooting himself and the other for fighting with a sergeant. He would receive a hardship discharge in 1959, claiming his mother needed care. He was discharged into the marine reserve.

There have been several misconceptions about Oswald's time in the marines. One was he was trained to speak Russian by the United States government. Though not trained by the government, the government did test his proficiency in Russian and found his Russian to be rudimentary. The reality is his Russian was self-taught. The other misconception was his shooting ability. He was sold to the American public as a sniper, a marine trained sharpshooter with the ability to carry out such a feat. Unfortunately, the rank he had at the time of his discharge was marksmen, the lowest score given.

In October 1959, Oswald departed the United Stated with only one thing on his mind to become a Russian citizen. He was a communist. The Russian's turned him down and asked him to leave. Desperate and angry, he tried to kill himself. The Soviets delayed his departure due to his self-inflicted wounds. He was held in a Moscow hospital in the psychiatric ward. By the end of the month, he was released by the hospital, and he entered the American Embassy to discuss renouncing his citizenship. During his interview with officer Edward Snyder, he insinuated he had information of interest for the Russians and was going to share it with them. Snyder found his interaction with Oswald disturbing but did not accept his renouncement. Oswald, infuriated, in a fit threw his passport at Snyder and stormed out of the embassy.

Lee was a great propaganda event for the Soviets, An American defecting to the Soviet Union. He was provided with a job at a Russian electronic company making TVs and radios and an above-average apartment. They even provided a tutor to teach him the Russian language. He was kept under constant surveillance.

By 1961 Russia's luster had faded. Most of us have all heard about his wife Marina but what most of us don't know is she was his consolation prize. His heart belonged to one of his coworkers, Ella German. In January 1961, he proposed, and she declined. Shortly thereafter, he began reconsidering his decision to stay in Russia. He reached out to the United States Embassy in Russia and requested the return of his passport. At about the same time, he meets his wife, Marina Prusakova.

They would marry six weeks after meeting. By June 1, 1962, he had become a father and received a repatriation loan from the United States. He and his young family departed Russia for a new life in the United States. Oswald had envisioned press coverage and some celebrity upon his return to the United States. He was sorely disappointed with the press coverage he and his family received.

The young Oswald family settled in Ft. Worth, Texas. During the seventeen-month period prior to the assassination of JFK, Oswald fluttered about. He was unable to keep a job for very long. He became entangled directly and indirectly with David Ferrie, Guy Bannister, Jack Martin, Clay Shaw, Carlos Marcello, Santos Trafficante, Sam Giancana. All of the previously named figures have all come under suspicion as being figures, directly and indirectly, involved in JFK's assassination.

David Ferrie

Guy Bannister

Jack Martin

Clay Shaw

Carlos Marcello   Santos Trafficante Jr.   Sam Giancana

The Oswalds separated in the late spring of 1963. His wife and daughter resided in Dallas, Texas, and Oswald returned and settled in New Orleans. He would eventually reconnect with his old commander from his civil air patrol days in 1955, David Ferrie.

David Ferrie (second from left) and a teenage Lee Harvey Oswald (far right) in a group photo of the New Orleans Civil Air Patrol in 1955

David Ferrie was involved with the CIA and Carlos Marcello. He also worked with Guy Bannister as a private investigator. It was through Ferrie that Oswald met Bannister and became involved with "Fair play for Cuba." Fair play for Cuba was based out of Bannister's office.

Less than 60 days prior to the assassination, in October 1963, Oswald returned to Dallas and lived in a rented room in the Oak Cliff area of Dallas. His wife and children lived in Irving, Texas. He lived in Dallas during the weekdays and with his family on weekends. On October 15, 1963, Oswald was hired at the Texas School Book Depository. As the saying goes, "the rest is history," or is it?

One thing is certain there are so many loose ends to the assassination and Oswald's actual role in it. There is a missing piece to the puzzle. Given my father was ordered to be at a specific location on November 22, 1963, along with several others, it is obvious our government had knowledge of what was to unfold that day and, more importantly, had a hand in it. It was a coordinated operation with several individuals and groups involved – groups that, under normal circumstances, would never cooperate with each other. Politics make for strange bedfellows. Oswald, knowingly or unknowingly, in the middle of these coordinated efforts, took the fall and paid the price.

Chapter 15: Nixon, Watergate, Bell Mortgage, Costa Rica

My junior year in high school could have been called my year of enlightenment. I had already learned that contrary to the history books we were made to study, JFK was not killed by some lone nut but by a conglomerate of people. Obviously, I was studying modern American history and government, which made it such a joy to have discussions with my father. The best way to explain it is; if the history book said "X," he would say "A," blowing the history book out of the water. Great to know, but it did absolutely nothing from an academic standpoint for me.

If you think JFK was the only president that was to be taken out for political motivation, then you are wrong. Richard Nixon was also a possible target for the political chess game being played regarding Cuba. When the subject of Watergate came up in my studies, a whole new can of worms opened right up.

Richard Nixon

I already knew that whatever my parents had to tell me about Nixon and Watergate, I probably couldn't submit to my teacher just like the whole JFK assignment. You would think I would have opted not to ask them, but no, I was going to jump in with both feet. Little did I know what a tale I would get.

My father was home, and when I got in, I asked him about Nixon, and he just gave me a smile. You know that smile the Cheshire cat's smile from Alice in Wonderland makes? Well, that's the smile I got from him. He said he would share his experiences concerning Nixon after dinner, which translated to me that this was going to be a late night.

There I was, sitting in our living room on the leather chair my mom normally sits on with pen and paper in hand, waiting for yet another history lesson. My dad grabbed a beer and sat down in the other leather chair and asked me what was it I needed to know about Nixon. I told him we were studying Nixon and Watergate, but I was more interested in the comment he made about another president being taken out. "Was the Watergate scandal what you meant?"

He laughed and said no, not directly, but it would end up there. He said Nixon was elected president at the end of the 1960s, and one of his promises was to end the Vietnam war, but what the average American doesn't understand is war is a huge source of money. There were very large American companies with government contracts providing weapons, commodities, and services to the war. It really was in the best financial interest of those companies and the country not to just shut it down. So, the war went on. The war went on, the mission to get Castro wasn't at the forefront anymore.

I asked him what he was doing during that time. He stopped for a moment and answered, "Running guns and agents into Cuba. The Blockade did its job; it caused shortages of commodities on the island. That created a need for commodities, medicine, diapers, everything you can go to the grocery store for, but you cannot get there anymore. This opened the door for us to begin taking in these items to the island through their ports. Our boats were being escorted into the port by Castro's own Patrol boats." "Wait," I said, "STOP! Why would they let you do that?"

He said it is really very simple. "Everyone on the island was hungry; they had no money, they had limited supplies, and that's all it takes. The revolution had failed; all that was promised was not realized, and instead, they were living in poverty. That will drive anyone into doing what they have to do to better their situation. Besides, they thought we were just bringing in commodities and a person here and there that were there to see family who was still living on the island. In return, they were paid. We even bought lobsters; all of this was done with fishing boats.

Well, the operation was very successful, but several operatives wanted things to move along faster. They wanted Castro out. The bastard had been in power for a decade; they wanted him out no matter what the cost. Through this operation, several of Castro's men turned and were now working for us, and we got our hands on a Cuban Patrol Boat. Those operatives within the operation began to formulate a plan.

They recruited within the organization. The plan was moving forward; money was being spent, planes purchased. The plan involved missiles...."

I said, "MISSILES?"

He said, "Yes. In short, there were going to be two missiles shot at the same time; one an aircraft flying over the base in Guantanamo and the other at Nixon's Key Biscayne house. For the best effect, Nixon would have to be at the Key Biscayne house when it happened. He shrugged his shoulders and just looked at me."

I sat there for a moment, speechless. Then I said, "Wait, how could you do both at the same time?" He smiled and said, "The missile that would hit the military base would come from a Cuban military aircraft. One of Castro's Military men was now one of us and was charged with that task. The other would come from the Cuban Patrol Boat we had acquired. Obviously, the boat would have to be within a few miles of Key Biscayne to hit its target, and it would immediately be found after the launch.

"The hit would have all the markings of a Cuban attack which would cause an immediate retaliation by the US. I said, "What about Russia? That was the beauty of the whole thing, publicly Cuba attacked, eventually they would realize that was not what actually happened, but by that time, the official story would allow them to stand down and save political face. The entire situation, including the death or capture of Castro, would last all of 24, maybe 48 hours and Cuba would be liberated and under US control."

I knew this conversation wasn't going to be a simple conversation like most of my classmates would have with their parents, but I had no idea this was the conversation I would have. I looked at my dad and said, "I know JFK was very well hated and made a lot of enemies but Nixon? Was he just as loathed? No, it wasn't personal like Kennedy. Kennedy was very personal. Nixon would have been collateral damage. Besides, he said it would have been a much better reason for a Vice President to become President than Watergate."

"Nixon wasn't personal. If it was personal, there was plenty of opportunity to take him out." He recalled an incident during this time when there were several fishing boats loaded with weapons moored along the Miami River, ready to move out. When a boat came by, it was Nixon on the boat. There he was in the middle of operatives and weapons, and he had no idea. If it was personal, it would have been very easy to take him and everyone on that boat out," he said

I got up, and my dad said, "No, no, no, sit down. I am not done." I said, "Okay, I need to get a drink of water." I walked to the kitchen, poured myself a glass of water, and tried to digest all that was just said. At that moment, all I could think about was why can't my family be normal. I walked back to the living room and sat down.

Well, I looked at my dad and said, "Well, obviously, none of this happened." He said, "No, it didn't." I asked, "Who pulled the plug?" He responded, "Manuel and others." I then asked, "Why didn't it happen? There were a few too many unknowns. If Castro's Military men weren't able to do their part, it would bring into question the hit on Nixon's house. Too many people already had a question about the hit on JFK. We did not need to deal with another president's death investigation leading back to its own government directly or indirectly." I asked, "Were you involved?" He said, "No, not directly."

"Not directly?" I asked. He said, "No. I was not directly involved, but funding for this and other operations came from the company indirectly along with funds provided by private parties with a vested interest in seeing the Castro Government removed from power." I remember saying, "So you collected donations? I can just imagine that; just like in church, here comes the offering basket, and someone with thousands of dollars would just dump it in there for you guys." He laughed and said, "No, not just like that."

He said, "After the mess with Aranzazu, money sources began to dry up. Direct funding wasn't as easily acquired, so we had to figure out how to get indirect funding sources. Now, some people's entire participation with these operations was money. They couldn't get their hands dirty, but they contributed by providing funding, "El Gran Senior" (a high-profile Cuban Exile) was one, and others provided money in exchange for services and other things of need. Miami was full of fake businesses that were all fronts for money to be laundered for operations. Make no mistake the company was fully aware of them and their purposes. Guns don't come for free they have to be bought, gas has to be paid for and operatives have to be paid—" I interrupted him and said, "Isn't this about the time we moved to Costa Rica?"

He replied, "Yes. Toni and I were caught running guns to Cuba. It wasn't just the guns but also the source of our funding, and others were exposed. We had to leave. It wasn't a choice; I was re-assigned along with Toni. We were sent to deal with the Sandinistas in Nicaragua to avoid the shit storm that was going to come down."

"What shit storm?" I asked.

"While all of this was going down the Watergate scandal hit, changes within "the company" began shutting down operations. It was not an easy time." Finally, I said, "Watergate." He said, "You know the basics; there was a break into the democratic party's office. Some files were taken and offices wired. The wires didn't work, so the idiots went back and broke in again to fix the problem; that was their mistake. They got caught. The break-in wasn't that bad. It was what Nixon did after it that killed him. No different than if I get caught the company is going to deny knowing anything about me and my activity, Nixon denied any knowledge and involvement with break-in. Had he just thrown some simple misinformation out there, it all would have been buried. Instead, he not only denied it but recruited the company to head off the Feds. That was far worse than the actual break-in he was trying to deny.

The more people involved in trying to clean up his mess, the more of a mess he made. During the investigation, it was discovered Nixon had been taping all discussions that were made in the president's office since the day he took office. Well, not only did that cause alarms to go off throughout the intelligence community, but now those tapes became a target by those investigating Watergate as the smoking gun to prove his involvement. It had gone from a blundered burglary into an intelligence fiasco. It was the discovery of those tapes existence that sealed his fate. Everyone was running scared."

So, I said, "Why Costa Rica and not Nicaragua?" He said, "Simple, Costa Rica was safe, and we had family there. Your mother, you, and your brother wouldn't be alone." "Why didn't Toni's wife and kids go?" I asked. He sighed and said, "His wife refused to go. This was his mess, and she was done with it. Your mom, your grandparents, and the whole family weren't at all happy about the situation. We moved to Costa Rica, and you guys had a whole new world to deal with, but those left in Miami had to deal with the repercussions of this mess. That's why when we moved back to the States, it was to California, not Miami. That's one of the reasons why you and your brother didn't go to Miami for several years."

I asked Dad about our home in Miami. I know Tia Ana and Tio Arturo own the house now, and I asked him how did that come to be. He said, "They bought the house." I told him I had heard him and mom fighting about the house on a few occasions, and her saying she didn't care; that it was dirty money and she didn't want it. I asked him what that was all about. He said that was part of the mess, but not something he wanted to go into at the moment. It would take too long to explain. He said, "That's a conversation for another time; it's really late, and you have to go to bed."

Richard Nixon was the gift that kept on giving. Not only did he hire the gang that couldn't shoot straight to pull off Watergate, but then he kept stepping in shit every time he tried to fix the mess he made. I'm sure when it was all said and done with him, those operatives must have thought in retrospect they should have executed the plan to take him out.

My father wasn't kidding; Miami was a hotbed for fake fronts for laundering money for covert operations and drugs.

Though my father never involved himself in the drug trade, several ex-operatives and others did. Among the fronts, my father used was Bell Mortgage.

Bell Mortgage Corporation was a mortgage company founded by Andres Castro in 1969 per Florida Divisions of Corporation. During my research, it appears he was approached about using his company and developing other companies as fronts to launder money for covert operations. The long and short of it was inflate the values of the properties being put up for mortgages. The extra money generated by this practice was passed on to the company for operations. These funds were for operations in Central and South America, extracting Fidel's influence and the spread of communism at our country's back door. The other companies that involved my father used as fronts were; American Continental Trading Company Co., Bell Mortgage Corp. of Hialeah, Inc., Onyx Finance, Inc., Krista Enterprises, Inc.

As for my childhood home, its mortgage was through Bell Mortgage. All the arguments my parents had, and comments made about our home and the proceeds from it as dirty money finally made sense. Sometime in late 1974, after my father was caught running guns, it all came crashing down. A multitude of arrests for mortgage fraud, among other charges, flew around Miami. Among those arrested was Andres Castro.

Detail by Officer/Registered Agent Name

Florida Profit Corporation
KRISTA ENTERPRISE, INC.

Filing Information

Document Number	441671
FEI/EIN Number	00-0000000
Date Filed	12/12/1973
State	FL
Status	INACTIVE
Last Event	CANCEL FOR NON-PAYMENT
Event Date Filed	09/03/1976
Event Effective Date	NONE

Principal Address

990 S.W. FIRST ST.
MIAMI, FL

Mailing Address

990 S.W. FIRST ST.
MIAMI, FL

Registered Agent Name & Address

ZAIAC (MANUEL)
150 S.E. 2ND AVE.
SUITE 610
MIAMI, FL

Officer/Director Detail
Name & Address

Title PD

FERNANDEZ (OSCAR)
MIAMI, FL

Title ST

RODRIGUEZ (JOSE A.)
MIAMI, FL

Title D

RODRIGUEZ (JOSE A.)
MIAMI, FL

Title D

YGLESIAS (GUILLERMO J.)
MIAMI, FL

Annual Reports
No Annual Reports Filed

Krista Enterprises, Filing Information

Detail by Officer/Registered Agent Name

Florida Profit Corporation
ONYX FINANCE, INC.

Filing Information

Document Number	439733
FEI/EIN Number	00-0000000
Date Filed	11/14/1973
State	FL
Status	INACTIVE
Last Event	CANCEL FOR NON-PAYMENT
Event Date Filed	09/03/1976
Event Effective Date	NONE

Principal Address

3383 N.W. 7TH ST.,
MIAMI, FL

Mailing Address

3383 N.W. 7TH ST.,
MIAMI, FL

Registered Agent Name & Address

ZAIAC (MANUEL)
150 S.E. 2ND AVE., SUITE 610,
MIAMI, FL

Officer/Director Detail

Name & Address

Title PD

CASTRO(ANDRES)
MIAMI, FL

Title VD

YGLESIAS (GUILLERMO)
MIAMI, FL

Title S

ANTON (URBANO E.)
MIAMI, FL

Title D

ANTON (EDUARDO)
MIAMI, FL

Annual Reports

No Annual Reports Filed

Onyx Enterprises, Filing Information

Detail by Entity Name

Florida Profit Corporation
AMERICAN CONTINENTAL TRADING CO.

Filing Information

Document Number	306142
FEI/EIN Number	00-0000000
Date Filed	06/15/1966
State	FL
Status	INACTIVE
Last Event	CANCEL FOR NON-PAYMENT
Event Date Filed	09/03/1976
Event Effective Date	NONE

Principal Address

3383 N.W. 7TH ST.
MIAMI FL.

Mailing Address

3383 N.W. 7TH ST.
MIAMI FL.

Registered Agent Name & Address

ZAIAC, MANUEL
150 S.E. 2ND AVE.
SUITE 610
MIAMI FL. 33131

Officer/Director Detail

Name & Address

Title PD

CASTRO, ANDRES
3383 N.W. 7TH ST.
MIAMI FL.

Title VD

YALESIAS, GUILLERMO I.
3383 N.W. 7TH ST.
MIAMI FL.

Title SD

REQUEIO, ADOLFO
3383 N.W. 7TH ST.
MIAMI FL.

Title TD

BELTRAN, LUIS A.
3383 N.W. 7TH ST.
MIAMI FL.

Annual Reports

Report Year	Filed Date
1973	11/29/1973

Document Images

No images are available for this filing.

Detail by Officer/Registered Agent Name
Florida Profit Corporation
BELL MORTGAGE CORP. OF HIALEAH, INC.

Filing Information

Document Number	443405
FEI/EIN Number	00-0000000
Date Filed	02/08/1974
State	FL
Status	INACTIVE
Last Event	CANCEL FOR NON-PAYMENT
Event Date Filed	09/03/1976
Event Effective Date	NONE

Principal Address
2900 W. 12TH AVE. SUITE 23
HIALEAH, FL

Mailing Address
2900 W. 12TH AVE. SUITE 23
HIALEAH, FL

Registered Agent Name & Address
ZAIAC, MANUEL
150 SE 2ND AVE. SUITE 610
MIAMI, FL 33131

Officer/Director Detail
Name & Address

Title P

ARANGO, SIXTO
HIALEAH, FL

Title VD

REQUEJO, ADOLFO
HIALEAH, FL

Title SD

YGLESIAS, GUILLERMO
HIALEAH, FL

Title D

ARANGO, SIXTO R.
HIALEAH, FL

Annual Reports
No Annual Reports Filed

Bell Mortgage of Hialeah, Filing Information

Not only did Mr. Castro sing like a canary about the company's involvement in his company and all the other companies he helped develop. In April 1975, he filed a civil suit in Federal District Court suing the Central Intelligence Agency, its former directors; Richard Helms and William Colby, along with Guillermo Iglesias and Antonio Yglesias.

Aside from having to deal with the Feds showing up at their front door, my grandparents, Maggie, and other relatives had to deal with process servers trying to find my father. An article in the San Francisco Examiner on April 6, 1975, stated my father's whereabouts were, "whereabouts unknown." All of this was part of the shit storm that facilitated our move to Costa Rica.

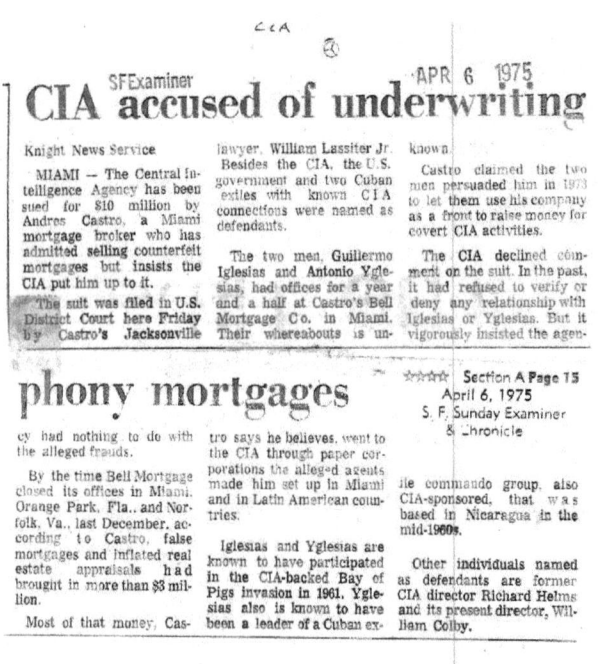

San Francisco Examiner April 6, 1975 Article

Chapter 16: The Dating Game & A Family Affair

Along with everything else that happened in my junior year of high school, my dad's role changed. He ceased being Mr. Mom. He had gotten a management position with a large detergent company. Life was really looking normal. As it was looking more normal, I really wanted to be like the girl next door. I wanted to go out with my friends and go out on dates. It really does suck being the oldest; it sucks even worse when you're a female, and if that isn't bad enough, the oldest and a female and the daughter of a Cuban male. All of that made it extremely difficult to get out.

I began asking to go out, and for a long time, the answer was. "No, we need you to take care of your sister." What? They were going to be home, so why the heck did they need someone to watch my sister? Answer; they didn't want me out yet. I persistently asked for six months, and finally, they let me go out with my friend Cheri to a party. I was so excited.

In Los Angles, high school parties in the mid-1980's contained the following ingredients:

- Someone's backyard or house (parents were normally out of town)
- A D.J.
- A few kegs of beer

- Teenagers from the age of 15 to about 19 years old

The mix added up to absolute chaos. I heard about them, but the first time I was let out of my little controlled environment was mind-blowing.

Cheri and I left my house in her 240Z and proceeded to a party where she met up with her boyfriend. Shortly after arriving, most of the party-goers were a bit looped. I was not looped. Yes, I had one wine cooler, but I was nowhere near the inebriation of my friend. Sometime later, she would argue with her boyfriend while the party was being broken up by police. Now, it was my thought; the party is over, time to go home, right? NOPE! Apparently, once the party breaks up, everybody would go to the local Carl's Jr. and meet again. We followed suit, with Cheri's boyfriend driving her car because she wasn't in any condition to drive any of us. As we arrived at Carl's Jr., once again, my friend and her boyfriend would begin to argue. As the scene progressed, somehow, she got a hold of her keys, got behind the wheel of her car. While I was in the passenger seat, she proceeded to burn out (spinning tires) and headed straight for a brick wall! Lovely, just what I always wanted to be part of a brick wall! The car came up to abrupt stop inches from the wall. That was the icing on the cake for me. I was ready to go home. We got back in the car, again her boyfriend behind the wheel, when I noticed several other classmates following us in cars.

Apparently, once I was to be dropped off, they were all going to continue onto another party. Unbeknownst to me, it was decided they would caravan to my house. As we began in the general direction of my house, the electrical system of Z went out. Yep, no radio, no brake lights, and no lights; we were just what every cop that night was looking for.

As you can imagine, we were pulled over. Now it was well beyond my curfew, I was in the back of this 240Z hatchback (by the way, it is very uncomfortable), and there was a cop flashing his flashlight in my face. Between Cheri's boyfriend and his best friend (who was caravanning behind us) they convinced the cop to let us go by telling him we were just a few blocks away from our destination. Finally, I got home.

As I walked toward the front door, all I could think about was what I was going to tell my father. If I told him exactly what happened and why I was late, that would be the last time I would be let out! I told myself I would cross that bridge after I got through the door.

As I opened the door, I realized he was nowhere in sight! What luck! I turned on the T.V. to Saturday Night Live. I looked around, and it was just me downstairs. Then a chill went down my spine, and I went to the garage to see if his car was still there. My heart was pounding in my chest. I was praying he was not out looking for me. Good, his car was there! I was in the clear. A wave of relief flooded over me. That relief was short-lived as I heard someone coming down the stairs. As I came back in from the garage, I found it was our dog who had come down to greet me. I leashed her up and took her out for a short walk. As I rounded the corner, I found the entire caravan still there arguing as to who was going to drive. My jaw dropped; they were right underneath my parents' bedroom window! Within a matter of minutes, they were gone.

As I returned with the dog, I opened the door and found my dad in the living room. My heart jumped in my throat. He looked at me and asked how the night went; I said fine. He assumed I'd been home for some time. He didn't ask, and I didn't tell!

After all of the "drama" of my first adventure out on the teenage scene, you would have thought I'd decided not to do that again, right? Nope, I went a few more times. Each time we would meet with our boyfriends at the party as well as our friends. After a few times of going out as a group, I thought I would push my luck. I had been asked out on a date. So, like the Christians were fed to the lions, I was going to be fed to my parents, and I was doing the delivery! I can remember it like it was yesterday. It was a Thursday night, and I had gotten home from swim practice. My brother was upstairs, and my sister was asleep. Here was my chance.

I came down the stairs and posed the questions, "Ah, Mami, ah, Papi, I was wondering if I could go out tomorrow night to the movies." They both looked at me really funny as if they were waiting for the other shoe to fall. So, I dropped it; I had been asked out on a date. Before I could even finish my sentence, the answer was "no" in unison. I looked at both of them and said, "Come on." I looked at my mom and said, "You got married at eighteen. You mean to tell me that Prince Charming just came up and knocked on your door and said here I am," as I pointed at my father.

Lesson number one: never ever pose a question to a parent if you do not have the answer for it already; you will live to eat your words! My mother smiled and said, "Yes." I looked at her and said, "What do you mean yes? You mean to tell me Papi just walked up to your door, knocked on it, and said, here I am." She said yes again. I was so screwed!

I said, "Wait a minute! Both of you were engaged to other people when you met; you are so giving me a bogus line." She agreed, saying, "Yes, we were engaged to other people when we met." She was going to go into her explanation, and I sat down on the stairs because I knew it was going to be a long one. She said my father literally walked up to her front door and knocked on it. She answered the door and let him in. He was not there to see her. He was there on business to see my grandmother, her mom. I said, "Wait, stop! What business would Papi have had with your mother?"

My mother proceeded to tell me about my grandmother. Apparently, she had been working for the United States while she was still in Cuba. When Castro took over, her name was on the list to be rounded up for execution. She fled the country. She continued to work for the company out of Miami. She was working with my father's aunt, Sara – yes, Tia Sara! My father had really gone to my mother's house due to business, not to meet her. She was just the icing on his cake that day. Needless to say, both of them called off their engagements, and, well, they got married.

What a revelation; it runs in the dang family. I remember asking, "Is there anybody in our family that is not involved in this mess? Is there going to be someone else that is going to pop out of the woodwork that works for the company and is a family member? I guess the family that spies together stays alive together!"

Not only did I fail miserably in convincing them to let me out on a date, but I found out working for the company was a family affair. I stormed off to my room.

I came down a little later and found my dad still downstairs. I went into the kitchen to get a glass of water.

When I came out, my father asked me to sit down. He looked at me and told me he wanted to have a serious discussion with me. I thought, *great, it's going to be one of those Father-Daughter talks about boys*. I was way wrong; I was so far off the map that if I was Columbus, I would have sailed off the edge of the world!

He looked at me and said, "You are incredibly smart. You are smart and beautiful, a perfect combination." He went on to tell me, "You could do anything you want, never let anybody make you feel like you can't do something because you are a girl." I was staring at him, waiting for the boy talk and trying to make sense of what he was trying to say to me. Then it rolled out: "With your brain and looks, you could have a hell of a career with the company."

He said I had a knack for not taking "no" for an answer but turning it into a "how." He said my non-conventional way of thinking could take me far. The company is always looking for people like me. I did not know whether to take this as a compliment or to be outraged. As he kept talking, I shut out everything else he was saying. I was just thinking about what he had just said.

I looked at him and said, "I was going to pass on such an opportunity." I told him I enjoyed all the traveling we had done when I was little, but I really liked being almost normal, and that is what I wanted out of life. I told him I wanted to be like everybody else. I wanted to have a career, get married, and have children. At that moment, he clearly understood where I was coming from.

I said, "You know I have been lucky nobody had asked me about my life, why I moved around so much, and what my father did for a living." I told him someday, I was going to have to explain all of this to someone, and I had to hope and pray it would not scare him off. I don't think he had ever thought about that scenario. Our conversation evolved from possible recruitment to how I was going to deal with explaining all of this to a prospective suitor.

We talked for a while. We both came to the conclusion I did not have to say a word to any of them, just to the one I would marry. He said to me, "To that man, all of this would not matter; all that would matter is that he has you."

I still didn't get to go out on that date that following night, but it was okay with me. It was postponing the inevitable day I would have to explain this. Make no mistake, that day was going to come – the question was when?

On New Year's Day in 1959, Fidel Castro unofficially seized control of Cuba (he would not officially become prime minister until February 16, 1959). Fulgenco Batista fled the country to the Dominican Republic. Within days of seizing control, Castro began the cleansing of the island by rounding up, arresting, and executing those involved with Batista, the United States, anyone who politically opposed him, and anyone he pleased by labeling them as criminals/traitors. Within the first two months of 1959, as many as 500 executions, if not more, were performed.

In the early hours of his regime, a list of names was distributed of those citizens to be arrested; among those names was my Grandmother, Ana Matilde Tomeu De Varona. She was among the few female attorneys in the country, worked with the company, and was also married to an American. Within 24 hours of Castro taking control of the island, my grandparents were made aware her name was on the list. She would have to flee, leaving her three children behind. The children stayed behind in the care of their grandparents. Chapter three of this book describes my grandmother's flight and the subsequent flight of the children. What that chapter doesn't address is her continued work with 'the company.' My grandmother headed the Cruzada Feminina Cubana (Female Cuban Crusade). This exiled Women's group engaged primarily in anti-Castro; anti-communist propaganda activities also involved my father's aunt Sara. Well, Prince charming literally knocked on my mother's door, and as the saying goes, the rest is history.

As for my grandmother's story, well, that's an entirely different book altogether.

Chapter 17: Iran-Contra – The Summer Of 1987

Do you remember where you were in the summer of 1987? Well, I do. I joined my parents, who moved from the LA basin of California to Fresno, California. Yes, my family moved to cow town. There was absolutely nothing there outside of the university. This was and still is Agricultural USA!

On May 5, 1987, I walked through the front door of our home to find my dad on the sofa, intently watching TV. The Iran Contra televised congressional hearings had begun. Oh, joy, the charade for the American public had begun. As a 19-year-old living in America's breadbasket, I realized how naive the American public truly was (and continues to be). I knew about Iran Contra as far back as 1979, and I was only 11!

As I came through the front door, my father motioned to me to come to sit by him and watch the farce taking place on national television. For those who don't quite know exactly what Iran Contra was, how it started and what it evolved into, here it is in a nutshell:

The CIA had been running operations out of Nicaragua ever since Castro was a revolutionary in Cuba. This was all possible – thanks to our then-ally, the Nicaraguan Government of Anastasio Somoza, the president. Right about now, you're saying…wait a minute; you know that name. You should because I mentioned it a few chapters back. Yes, that is the very same Anatisio Somoza my father extracted from Nicaragua in 1979 after the socialist, Cuban backed and soviet financed Sandinista group took over the country.

In July 1979, when Somoza fled the country, President Jimmy Carter was in office; God bless him, he had zero experience in dealing with any form of government, let alone banana republics. Needless to say, he left an even bigger mess in the region than before he took office. However, that November, Ronald Reagan had won the election, and Ronnie was not going to allow another communist country at the United States back door. So, he made a commitment to aid the Contras, who were conducting a guerrilla war against the Sandinista government of Nicaragua. Well, the republican president's commitment did not fare well with the democratic majority of Congress and Senate. As usual, the political game was being played, and Nicaragua was the football.

In 1983 during Reagan's first term, the Congress and Senate took action to tie Reagan's administration ability to provide military support to the Contra's. Ronnie wasn't going to take no for an answer, so he figured out how.

The how was simple: Congress and Senate's new legislation was very specific in its wording as to who was prohibited from providing military support to the Contras, CIA, the defense department, or any other US department. Well, the National Security Council (NSC) was not explicitly covered by this new legislation and technically was not a US department, so it spearheaded the operations. In order to fund this project, the NSC raised private and foreign funds for the Contras. It was originally just a Central American operation to aid the Contras.

It originated as a basic operation: American planes dropping weapons (Missiles, Ak-47, machine guns, etc.) in the Nicaraguan jungle for the Contras. Planes would fly out of American airstrips; Arizona, Arkansas, California, Florida, and Mexico. As those planes returned, the American covert bases in Mexico who were acting as lookouts for these planes would let them know if it was clear to enter American airspace and continue to the base in the US, or not to proceed but to land until it was clear.

Right about now, you should be recalling my father's arrest coming over the California Mexican border after blowing up a covert American base and airstrip. At the beginning of the whole Contra operation, he was involved, and so were several of the same cast of characters from previous operations he was involved in, like Felix Rodriguez.

At the age of 11, I knew about Nicaragua, and throughout high school, the rest trickled out. Though I was aware of the Contra portion of the whole Iran Contra equation, I wasn't quite sure of Iran's part of it. So, as I sat there with my father, of course, I had to ask, "What does Iran have to do with Nicaragua?" He gave me a one-word answer; hostages. He was engrossed with the hearing at that moment, so he did not elaborate. I knew it had nothing to do with the American Embassy hostages In Iran back in 1981 as they were released when Reagan literally took office. So, what hostages was he talking about?

I waited, and after about two beers, I asked again. The answer I got was, "American hostages were being held in Lebanon by Iranian-funded terrorists. A deal was struck with Iran, which was involved in a war with Iraq at the time, for weapons. The US put stipulations on the weapons deal, which included the release of the American hostages, and the money from the sale of those weapons was used for funding the Contras." I asked, "And when was this?" He said, "The hostages were taken in 1982."

It took me a few minutes to take that in and put it in its proper place in my memory of events. I looked at him and said, wait didn't we have laws keeping us from selling weapons to Iran? He answered, "Yes. All of this was done without the "official" knowledge of the Congress and Senate, but they knew." I looked at him and said, So we sold them weapons, they paid for it, and our hostages came home. He said, "something like that, but it took years to bring the whole damn hostage thing to an end, and during that entire time, we were selling them weapons, and some of that money was siphoned off for the Contra operations."

I should have stopped asking questions, but I didn't. "So, if it was covert, done on a wink, how did it get out?" He growled, "A fucking journalist in Lebanon wrote an article about a month after the Sandinistas shot down one of the planes dropping weapons to the Contras. that opened up a can of worms. The US denied any involvement in the weapons to the Contras, but after the article's publication, there was no way to put the worms back in a can that was opened. Then there was the whole Mexican connection and DEA mess regarding Kiki Camarena (Enrique Camarena)."

I looked at him and said, "Kiki? Mexico?" I thought we were talking about Nicaragua. He said, "We are, but Mexico was up to their necks in this shit." He said, "Kiki ese pobre infeliz no sabía en la mierda se estaba metiendo (that poor unfortunate soul had no idea the shit he was getting into)." He quickly changed the topic as the hearings had come back on.

Now, these hearings went on for weeks. This meant if Dad was home, and so was I, we would be watching the hearings, and I would get even more information. There were accusations during the hearings of drugs being smuggled to pay for the weapons for the Contras, and yes, I couldn't just let that go. I confronted him. I said, "Wait, really? Drug trafficking? Are you kidding me?"??!!!! He told me; "listen, most of the pilots that were used were CIA pilots, the same pilots used on previous operations. Those pilots knew how to get in and out of the states, and yes, they worked as drug traffickers. This isn't the first time this has happened. It has gone on for decades, as far back as the Korean war. "I believe back then that it was opium," he said. Now, did I agree with it? No. Did I participate in that? No, not knowingly. "What the hell do you mean not knowingly?" I exclaimed. He gave me a look and said, "I was only physically involved in the Iran Contra operation briefly because your mom gave me a choice: you guys or them. When I was in Mexico, I did not know what plane had drugs on them or not. Everyone knew drugs was something I was against."

"I'll tell you something else after this thing went from the Contras and included Iran, lots of pilots and operatives were not happy. Iran were and are terrorist. Some of those pilots as well as operatives contacted Government officials, Senators and informed them of the Operations."

"What did they do?" I asked. He replied, "Not a fucking thing. The DEA and the CIA were not cooperating with one another at the time. Even if they were, the CIA was not going to share information on their pilots. Pilots were complaining but making a lot of money. Some of those pilots had huge drug smuggling operations here in the United States. Those pilots paid a lot of government officials off to keep their drug businesses going during this time." I said, "Government officials like senators?" He said, "I don't know if senators were paid. I wasn't there, but if I had to guess it would normally be local law enforcement, local and state government officials. Once all of that starts, it's just a matter of time before it would completely be exposed. Too many people know, and they will start slipping and talking. Once shit starts to leak, you can't stop it. "I told them this would be bad, and when it goes down, someone will be taking the fall – the music had started to play."

I had a confused look on my face. "What in the hell does music have to do with anything?" I barked at him. He said, "It's political musical chairs. When operatives are contacting government officials, senators, congressmen, etc., it's done to cover their asses. Most of these guys know a whole lot of information about not just this operation but several others. If they are pinched, then all of that will spill out along with the information that person knows and who they told knew, and they did nothing. Those who knew and did nothing would be left standing when the music stops and the chairs are taken."

"What do you mean you told them? Who are 'them'?" He answered, "I've spoken with North, Rodriguez, operatives, and others I've known for years. On a few occasions, they told me shit was getting out."

As the hearings dragged on, I watched them with a different set of eyes than most Americans. I knew most, if not every career politician in that room, knew or had some knowledge of all of this. Political theater for the masses acting appalled and shocked this was going on. A necessity if they were to retain the support of their voters back home that's all these hearings were about. As I watched this farce of a congressional investigation, I recognized one of the witnesses; it was Felix Rodriguez.

In the end, Oliver North, along with a handful of others, took the hit. He was convicted much like G. Gordon Liddy and his crew in the Water Gate scandal. After "paying his debt to society," he followed in the steps of G. Gordon Liddy as an author and conservative talk show host.

Iran-Contra, as the covert operation is commonly known, is the Reagan administration's secret missiles-for-hostages exchange with the Iranian government. It began as a covert effort to arm the Nicaraguan Contras. The Contras were a right-wing army partly created by the CIA to topple the country's Sandinista rebels, who took over the country during the uprising in 1979. The Contras operation was disguised/buried within the US Army's 82nd, and 101st Airborne Divisions staged maneuvers in Honduras. These maneuvers were to prepare for an unlikely invasion by neighboring Nicaragua's left-wing Sandinista government. It was during these maneuvers some of the military equipment that was certified as being destroyed in airdrops by civilian air charters somehow ended up with Contra's and other groups. These civilian air charters were under contract to the CIA; Southern Air Transport and Evergreen International Airlines were among the charter companies.

These activities went on unabated for about 10-24 months until the democratic-controlled US Congress banned any aid to the Contras with legislation known as the Boland amendments. These amendments were a series of amendments that were passed between 1982-1984 designed specifically at limiting US government assistance to the Contras in Nicaragua by the Defense Dept., the Central Intelligence Agency (CIA), or any other government "department" from providing any military aid to the contras. However, the Reagan administration found a way to skirt the Boland amendment while complying with the letter of the law by having the covert operation under the supervision of the National Security Council (NSC), a counsel is not a department of the government. Yes, it is a play on words, but words matter in legal context.

Oliver North, Lieutenant Colonel

Oliver North, at the time, was a lieutenant colonel in the Marine Corps working for Reagan's National Security Council. Under his tenure, the National Security Council secretly continued the arms shipments. In 1986, the crash of a privately owned and contracted C-123 aircraft in Nicaragua exposed the covert operation.

On October 5, 1986, a Fairchild C-123 cargo plane owned by Southern Air Transport piloted by Bill Cooper who had two other persons on board was shot down, killing the pilot and killing a crew member. There was a surviving crew member, Eugene Hasenfus, who was captured by the Sandinistas and paraded in front of the press.

The C-123 cargo plane that was shot down was previously owned by Barry Seals. Barry Seals was among the CIA Pilots involved in the Iran Contra project but was also a huge Cocaine trafficker for the Medellin Cartel. His operations were run out of Mena, Arkansas. It has long been speculated, several local Arkansas officials, including state top officials, had knowledge (on a wink) of Seals operation of Contra's, drugs, and guns. In 1984 the federal government finally shut his operations down and arrested him. That C-123 cargo plane, along with all other equipment, was confiscated by the United States government yet somehow was released to Southern Air, another CIA pilot-owned company.

Chapter 18: Castro Drug Lord

The 1970s and 80s in Miami were a hotbed for the drug trade. Everything from pot to cocaine flowed through Miami. The city was ground zero for the drugs wars. Crime was rampant. The crime in Miami was broadcasted across television sets in American homes on July 11, 1979, during the Dadeland shootings. I was eleven at the time, and my brother and I were spending our summer vacation in Miami. I saw the news that evening and remember my grandparents telling us we were not allowed outside of the condominium complex under any circumstance.

Four years after the Dadeland shootings, Miami and the Cuban exile community would gain national attention – just not in some news story broadcasted across our TVs but from a movie, Scarface. The movie depicted the Marielle boat lift, Mariellitos becoming drug traffickers and dealers. It also would shine a bright light on the Colombian drug Cartels as the root of the problem. Scarface was so detrimental to the image of the Cuban exile community of Miami that during its filming, the cast and crew moved filming out of Miami due to increasing protests of the Cuban community and Miami Tourist Board. Fresh off the heels of Scarface came the television series Miami Vice.

Yes, it was the era of drugs, florescent fashion, cigarette boats, thongs, and synthetic music! My school's student body wore fluorescent shirts and found Miami Vice to be a direct reflection of the reality of Miami. I wore those same florescent fashions, including my Sheena Easton style hairstyle, along with all of my classmates. The guys in my class would walk around imitating Al Pacino's character "Tony Montana" or Don Johnson's character, "Sonny Crockett."

It was wonderful to walk the halls of my high school in California to friends calling out to me, "Say hello to my little friend." I took it in stride; what else was I supposed to do? I, along with my friends, saw both of those productions for what they were: entertainment, but the Cuban exile community didn't see it that way. Oddly enough, my dad also saw it as entertainment. It was during a Friday night episode of Miami Vice that led to a conversation.

It was during one of the multiple scenes of boat chases that my dad started smirking so much, I had to turn, look at him, and say, "Papi, please, I'm trying to watch TV." He told me if I didn't like it, I could go to my room. He said I could watch it in my own room if it bothered me so much. So, I got up, went up the stairs, and watched the episode in my room. It was Friday night, so I didn't have to be at school or practice the next morning. That said, I could stay up late, going downstairs to grab a snack to munch on while watching the episode.

My dad was right where I left him in his leather chair, finishing his beer. The eleven o'clock nightly news had just started. As I crossed the room in front of him on my way to the kitchen, he stopped me and asked me to sit down. Luckily my back was to him, and he couldn't see me roll my eyes. As I turned around and walked back toward him, I knew my plans for the night had just flown out the window. He smiled as I sat down.

I looked at him with an expression like, well? My expression made him laugh. "I'm sorry," he said. He went on, "I shouldn't have done that, but I couldn't help myself. You do know that is all made for TV." I said, "Except for the fact the crime and drug problems in Miami are true." As he took a drink from his beer, he said, "Yes, you're right."

"Too bad Hollywood doesn't play the political game," he said with a hint of cynicism. "Too bad Nixon, Ford, and the fucking Peanut Farmer ignored the problem and allowed it to flourish. They turned their heads and ignored Castro, and now they want to cry out about the drug problem and all the crime that comes with it. All of them were too scared to call a spade a spade after the Cuban Missile crisis. If they had shined the light on Castor's drug activities, a lot of things would be different. Castro was and is the biggest Narco-Trafficante (Drug Smuggler) of all."

I turned to him and said, "Papi, you mean Columbia is the smuggler of drugs?"

"No, No," he said, "Fidel Castro...." His pointer finger pointed straight up indicating the number one as he said, "He is the premier drug smuggler in this region of the world. He has been involved in drug trafficking since he took power. Un tipo (a guy) named Perez, a well-known marijuana farmer, did business with Castro before he took power and was named a hero of Castro's revolution.

"Castro lies to everyone, to the world, to the Cubans. Cuba has no industry to speak of anymore. Cuba's biggest product was sugar and tobacco. It once was the king of those markets; that's gone."

I chirped out, "The Russians help Cuba."

"The Russians give Cuba very little. The Russians don't need Cuba for anything. They helped Cuba just to have a toe in the area and to annoy the United States. No mi amor (my love), without the money from drug smuggling, Castro and his revolution would be dead," he retorted.

I gave him a stern look and said, "Embargo." He interrupted me before I could even finish. "Do you really think the "embargo" is the reason his revolution has failed? The main reason it has failed is that all of the educated Cubans left the island. All of the businesses were taken over by Castro and run by him. He has no mind for business. He has a mind for power, greed, and glory. The "embargo" doesn't affect Castro; it affects the Cubans. Castro and his government get anything they want regardless of the "embargo". They have business fronts in Panama that buy all the items they want. That's also where they run their drug money through: Panama."

This conversation had changed into a bit of a sparring match between Dad and me at this point. I stood up and said in a challenging manner, "And you know this for a fact, do you?" As soon as those words came out of my mouth in that specific tone, I knew I had crossed a line I should not have. From the smirk on his face, I knew the answer to the question I just posed was an overwhelming one, yes! Of course, he knew for a fact, and I, as his daughter should have known, but as a smart-ass teenager, I was looking to provoke him. I was defiant with that comment. The smirk he gave me also let me know he was locked, loaded, and was going to unleash on me! I thought to myself, *why didn't you just keep your mouth shut? You would be upstairs in your room watching TV.* Now I was in for a long night sparring with my father about a topic I thought I had the upper hand on. I was wrong.

Dad nodded and said, "Okay, okay. Yes, I do now for a fact. You do remember our conversation about Nixon?" I nodded my head yes. "You remember we were running guns into Cuba under the guise of bringing much-needed items, like diapers, food, etc.?" Again, I nodded yes. "Okay, we would bring our boats into Habana or Varadero. The officers we dealt with told us all about it. Nothing happens on that island without the Castros knowing about it or profiting from it. They knew we were there bringing items into the country; they obviously didn't know my real name or about the guns, but they knew to a certain extent the merchandise being brought in. Those very same officers not only escorted us in but would escort us out and would inform us where the US Coast guard was so we could avoid them. That was part of the service they provided us. They also provided those same services to the Colombians.

"I was told by those officers that planes would come into Cuba loaded with cocaine. Those planes would be offloaded, and the cocaine would be loaded onto waiting boats primarily out of the port of Varadero. Boats would also come into the port loaded with cocaine. They would refuel and rest there. Once the boats were ready to leave for South Florida with their drug shipment, the Cuban Navy would escort the boats into international waters and give the boat captains the coordinates of the US Coast guard in order to avoid them. Planes loaded with drugs were allowed to enter Cuban airspace, and Cuban traffic controllers would let them know if it was safe to continue on or to land. All of it was done for a price. All of it was done under the direct supervision of

Raul's Minister of the Armed Services y ese pedazo de mierda de Barabaroja (that piece of shit red beard).

"I was there several times and watched the boats being escorted out. When we were in Costa Rica, I was working in Nicaragua, and the Sandinistas were buying weapons with money provided by Cuba from their drug smuggling operations. I would meet with contacts for payment for the arms in Panama. Cuba funneled all of its drug money through Panama. Panama, Noriega's banking system allowed for all of this, okay? Cuba had companies set up all over to circumvent the embargo, and most if not all the money would go through Panamanian banks. All of it was bought and sold with American dollars through those banks, all of it with the knowledge of the American Government.

"The Castro brothers hasta aqi en la mierda de Drogas (up to their necks in drugs)," he motioned with his hand across his neck. "Most of the money is to finance all of Castro's foreign illegal enterprises, assist Cuba's economy, and finance Fidel and Raul's Lifestyle. Everyone on that island starves while those *hijos de puta* (sons of bitches) live the high life.

"Every single one of the naval officers and Cuban coast guard officers we worked with were disillusioned with the Castro brothers. They all realized they were no better than Batista; in fact, they said the Castro brothers were worse.

Pobre pasa hambres (poor starving people)." He finally took a breath.

I nodded and thought to myself, *Red Beard*. Yep, that's a pirate's name. Red Beard was helping Castro smuggle drugs into the United States. I wanted to say, 'So, are Peter Pan and tinker bell involved too?' But I knew that would set him off, and I would be stuck in that leather chair for hours if I did that. I looked at him said, "Good night, Papi." He wished me good night and told me he would be going to bed as soon as he finished his beer.

In the summer of 1989 in Clovis, California, this conversation would be revisited. It was Saturday, and I had been out all day on my boyfriend's boat. I came through the door to find my parents in their living room. They were discussing that evening's news. As I walked through the house to the bathroom, I overheard something about a Cuban General on trial. After I showered, I joined them in the living room. They were still discussing the same topic.

For a bit of fun, I jumped into the conversation. I said, "what about Cuban General on trial? How did we catch him?" My dad said, "We didn't catch him. Cuba has the general on trial." Well, that comment threw me for a loop. I said, "Why in the hell would our news care about a general on trial in Cuba?" He replied, "Castro's little drug business finally was exposed." My mom got up announced she was tired and was going to take a bath. Knowing full well, my father was talking in riddles to engage me in this conversation. I quashed his riddles with, "So, Fidelito's drug smuggling is exposed, and a general is on trial in Cuba. This means what to me?"

That comment was the equivalent of taking the first shot across his bow. He got up, went into the kitchen, grabbed a beer, and came back into the room. I laughed, and so did he; we both knew where the conversation was going. "Papi, before you start, can I get the short version because I'm tired?" He said, "Yes," then continued to say after a pause, "if there is one thing Castro hates is being embarrassed on the international stage. For almost twenty years, the Cuban government has been accused of facilitating drug smugglers, and Fidel would respond to it as "Yankee Propaganda.""

Recalling our previous conversation with him regarding Castro the Drug Lord, I remembered him telling me Fidel used the drug money for weapons. Given the times we were in, I couldn't help myself and went on to say, "Well then Cuba has its own version of Iran Contra…the irony." My dad started laughing and nodded yes, and then I added: "Every country has its version of drugs for guns or other covert operations they want to fund." He laughed even harder. Then, with a straight face, I said, "So, this general is the patsy taking the fall." My father stopped laughing.

"Pobre Ochoa (poor Ochoa). You know he gave his life to those two bastards. He should have learned by seeing how Fidel got rid of Cienfuegos and Che. He should have known that when the music stopped playing, he would be left without a chair. Fidel couldn't allow himself or Raul to be implicated. Fidel has made numerous comments about how he has eradicated prostitution, gambling, and drugs from the island – he could not allow himself to be seen as betraying his own revolution. Eso dos come mierdas (those two idiots/assholes) got caught in a DEA operation." With that being said, we both got up and went to bed.

The next few weeks, I watched the news and saw it wasn't just General Ochoa. It was a multitude of officers that were on trial for a multitude of offenses, including drug trafficking and treason. General Ochoa was executed in July of that year. I remember asking my dad why Navy Admiral Santamaria did not get executed. He replied, "Santamaria struck a deal with the Castro brothers to take the blame; in return, his life was spared and his family taken care of. Ochoa never confessed; besides, he was a very popular revolutionary, and from my sources, after Gorbachev's changes, he was looking forward to Cuba following suit allowing for democracy to begin in Cuba. That is why Ochoa met the wall."

It's doesn't take a genius or boxes of evidence to see that the Castro regime was and always has been underfunded. In order to fund Cuba's dying economy, Fidel and his government resorted to drug trafficking and laundering money. Anyone with any common sense and eyes could see it. Unfortunately, common sense and eyes mean nothing to the American government and its constituency. The American public was and is the preverbal ostrich with its head in the sand, but why?

Researching Fidel and Raul's involvement in drug smuggling really wasn't all that hard. My father was right; they had been involved in the drug trade since they took over. Some of the names he mentioned were easy enough to find, but Red Beard – that was a different story. During the early days of the internet, if you typed in 'Red Beard,' you would get questions like, 'Did you mean black beard?' or the photographs of men with red beards. As the years passed, I dug deeper, and I finally found out who Red Beard was: Manuel Pineiro Losada.

Manuel Pineiro Losada aka Barabaroja

Like Fidel and Raul Castro, Manuel Pineiro Losada came from a very prosperous family. He was the son of a Bacardi executive. He was educated abroad; he attended Columbia University in New York. It was during his time there that his socialist views formed. As the story goes, he returned to Cuba in 1955 and was one of the founders of the "July 26 Movement." He fought alongside the Castro brothers and Che Guevara. The Barbudos (heavily armed bearded soldiers) were those selected to apprehend anyone associated with the Batista regime early on after the revolutionaries took power; he was among them. Aside from his loyalty to the cause, which was a trademark that would move him up Castro's political ladder, so was his red beard – hence the nickname Barabaroja (Red Beard).

From the very beginning, Barabaroja played a key role in building one of the most successful security agencies ever constructed. He served various functions early on in the Castro regime. During the Bay of Pigs Invasion, he was deputy to Ramiro Valdés Menéndez, head of G-2 (Seguridad del Estado, or state security). In 1961, he was appointed as the deputy minister of the interior and head of the so-called Technical Viceministerio, the body that would be later responsible for gathering intelligence and developing strategies to expand communism in Latin America. He was also the head of "El Departmento de Américas" (The Department of the Americas), which was in charge of sabotage and subversion.

As head of all Cuban operations in Nicaragua, El Salvador, the rest of Central and South America, along with the United States, he was responsible for providing funding for guerrilla weapons to spread Castro's revolution throughout the hemisphere. Funding was a problem, but a problem that was easily overcome by dealing drugs. Cuba's drug business funded; guns, government coffers, and the Castro brothers' pockets. As the head of these agencies, he answered directly to both Raul and Fidel Castro. He became one of the most influential and trusted figures within the Cuban government. So trusted was Barabaroja that it fell to him to inform Fidel Castro of Che Guevara's death in 1967.

Cuba has been engaged in the drug trade since the infancy of the Castro government. It originally came to light with the arrest of four people in Miami; Jose Barral, Mario Delgado, Jose Leone, and Gabriela Giralt. The foursome implicated their Cuban handler, Juventino Guerra who reported to Manuel Piñeiro Losada (Barabaroja). The United States publicly acknowledged the drug trafficking link, and as a result, Cuba was expelled from the Organization of the Americas (OAS) in 1962. In June of 1967, during the inquiry before the OAS, a Cuban-trained Venezuelan intelligence officer established before the world the Cuban link of drugs for weapons for revolutionary guerrillas in the hemisphere. The evidence provided a major connection between Habana, the guerrilla movements, and narcotics. The trend then and that is still in play today is; Cuban intelligence officers engage in and direct drug trafficking activities here in the United States of America. Barabaroja has been quoted many times, stating, "If the US drug war causes damage to the United States, so be it. Drug trafficking raises money for 'The Revolution."

In the 1970s, the primary objective of Barabaroja's Departmento de Américas was exporting the revolution. During this time, Cuba was providing training and weapons to Colombia's guerrillas (M-19). In 1975 a former Cuban intelligent agent, Fernando Ravelo Renedo, was named ambassador to Colombia. It was he who suggested to his superiors; Manuel Piñeiro Losada (Barabaroja), Raul Castro, and Fidel Castro the use of narcotics to finance the spread of the revolution. Ravelo was Columbia's Habana link and, as such, promised that he and the Cuban government would help both the guerrillas and the traffickers in their drug trafficking efforts, but it would come at a price.

In 1978, Cuba upped its involvement with narcotics by adding another Cuban intelligence department. The ministry of the interior, headquarters of Cuban intelligence, developed the MC Department under the direction of Colonel Tony De La Guardia. The sole purpose of this newly formed sub-agency was to find ways to raise foreign money for Cuban operations.

Why foreign currency, or to be exact, American dollars? It is really quite simple: the Cuban dollar back then, as it is today, has no value, and the American dollars is the world's reserve currency. Cuba resorted to old-style tactics; they took a page from the Italian mob's playbook. They created private companies in different parts of the world through which they could circumvent the "embargo" and conduct illegal business activities, including drug deals. Panama was where most of these companies conducted its business and banking, thanks to Manuel Noriega.

Panama was Cuba's offshore financial center that included offshore banks and various forms of shell companies for money laundering. Panama was also used by the drug cartels to move their money. The cartels paid the Cuban government for the use of airstrips, the port at Varadero, their airspace, Cuban naval/coastguard escorts, and for information giving the locations of the American authorities. Cash would be delivered to Cuba and or deposited into one of their shell companies' bank accounts in Panama. Cuba was a safe haven for traffickers.

An American Company called Everything Goes Inc., and its owner James Herring was operating in the area at the time, providing Cuba with merchandise that was banned through the "embargo". James was running computer equipment to Cuba using speed boats. According to Herring's testimony in front of the US Senate in 1985, he would go to Varadero with a load of equipment, and it would be received by Cuban gunboats. He would be escorted to the military dockage at Varadero, where they would offload. When he was ready to return to the Florida Keys, he said Cuban military vessels would escort him out. During his testimony, Herring stated he noticed that Cuban intelligence agents were handling narcotics. Through familiarity with some of those agents, Herring eventually realized that Cuba had significant amounts of drugs stored in warehouses on the scene near Varadero. The Herring testimony has been confirmed by others.

It was also during these congressional hearings that Juan Lozano, also known as Johnny Crump, a Columbian drug smuggler corroborated James Herring's testimony. He also provided further information on Cuba's involvement in the drug trade. Johnny Crump claimed he met the Ambassador of Cuba, Fernando Ravelo Renedo, in 1979 at a party in Bogota. Johnny floated the idea to him about refueling drug planes in Cuba – Ravelo liked the idea and presented it to the Castro brothers and Barabaroja. Crump also met with other officials from Barabaroja's Departamento de Las Americas, Gonzalo Bassols-Suarez, and between them, a plan was formed.

It began simple enough; A boat loaded with drugs left Columbia bound for Cuba, and Johnny Crump was bound for Cuba as well via a plane. Upon his arrival, he was taken to the Habana Libre hotel as a formal guest of the Cuban government. He met with Cuban officials; among them was Rene Rodriguez Cruz, a member of Cuba's Central Committee and another friend of Fidel Castro. After enjoying several days of Cuba's hospitality Crump was informed the drug load from Columbia had arrived. He was taken to Varadero, and there he met the Cuban Admiral, Aldo Santamaria. Santamaria told Crump that his Cuban naval vessels would protect drug shipments coming through Cuban waters in the future.

In January 1982, Johnny Crump was arrested at the Omni International Hotel in Miami on charges of importing marijuana and cocaine into the United States. He was indicted and tried in the Southern District of Florida. Crump collaborated with authorities and testified against several high-ranking Cuban government officials and Colombian smugglers. As a result of his testimony Santamaria, Rene Rodriguez Cruz, Ravelo Renedo, the Cuban Ambassador to Colombia, and Bassols, were likewise indicted.

Other witnesses who had infiltrated into the United States testified to the involvement of Cuba in the drug trade. Mario Estevez, a Cuban intelligence officer who was arrested in 1981, testified about the extensive drug ring Habana had developed. He admitted to personally accepting the operation to distribute over three hundred kilos of cocaine in the United States, originating from Cuba.

Smugglers rendered substantial assistance to the Middle District of Florida at the time. They testified they paid for protection through Cuban waters to the Cuban government. The payment was in the form of drugs and cash deposits into bank accounts in Panama. The Cuban Navy and Coast guard working with radio towers in the Florida Keys who would direct the smugglers' vessels as to the appropriate time and routes to avoid detection by the United States Coast Guard. As planes began to fly into Cuba, the Cuban government provided protection for a price. This information was released during the trial of Manuel Noriega, the former president of Panama.

Carlos Lehder, a drug smuggler, would testify he met with Raul Castro and other Cuban officials in 1982 to negotiate an agreement that would allow cartel pilots to fly drug-laden planes over Cuba on their way to the United States. He also stated his visit to Habana prompted Fidel to be more hands-on with Cuba's drug trade. The Castro brothers wanted a greater portion of the profits. They knew all the players, the producers, and the distributors. So a change in the business took place, and Cuba became a drug seller. In 1982 Manuel Pineiro Losada (Barabaroja) and General Osmani Cienfuegos arrived in Panama to coordinate intelligence and narcotic activities.

In July of 1983, Jose Raul Perez Mendez, a Cuban intelligence officer, defected. It was during his debriefings that he linked Raul Castro directly to drug operations. He added that Cuban intelligence had over three hundred intelligence officers engaged in espionage and drug trafficking in the United States. Another defector, General Rafael Del Pino of the Cuban air force, during his debriefing, testified he would give permission for the drug planes to fly through Cuban air space and land at Varadero only after he received authorization to do so. The authorization usually came from Raul Castro himself. He would allow certain planes to fly over sensitive areas. The drug flights were of common knowledge to the top tier in the Cuban Air Force. Everything was out in the open. Aside from the profit they were making, the objective was to flood the United States with as much cocaine as possible. A common quote of Fidel Castro was, "What you need to do is to whiten America with cocaine in order to destroy it."

Cuba's undoing would come in 1987. The Drug Enforcement Administration (DEA) was electronically monitoring the activities of two smuggling organizations operating between Colombia, Cuba, and Miami. The Ruiz organization was based in Miami, and the Ceballos organization operated in Colombia. Undercover agents had penetrated both organizations by monitoring their telephone conversations, using body wires, and videotaping operations. It was through this surveillance and recordings the DEA became aware of a fellow by the name of Reinaldo Ruiz. Reinaldo had connections inside the Cuban government, a cousin by the name of Miguel Ruiz Poo.

Ruiz openly discussed his connections on tape. He mentioned relatives who had access to Cuban government officials they could guarantee the security of cocaine shipments as they moved through Cuba. His son Ruben, a pilot, flew the planes, and he was in charge of refueling in

Cuba. According to Ruiz, cigarette boats would cross the Florida Straights and make land on the Cuban coast at DIA Varadero, near the lighthouse. These boats would be directed by the Cuban Coast Guard Colonel, by the name of Pardo, to take the boats up a creek where a number of cigarette boats used by drug smugglers were moored. Those boats were secured and guarded by Cuban Coast Guard personnel. Meanwhile, Reinaldo's son Ruben picked up the cocaine in Colombia and would fly it to Cuba. As he approached Cuban airspace, he would be directed to the Varadero airport. The cocaine was unloaded by Cuban military personnel, taken to the Cuban Coast Guard safe houses, and loaded onto the Miami-bound speedboats.

On February 23, 1988, Reinaldo Ruiz, a drug smuggler, along with fifteen others were indicted for smuggling cocaine through Cuba, Haiti, and the Turk and Caicos Islands. DEA detained Ruiz along with his wife, a Cuban national, on February 28, 1988. Ruiz's wife was a nineteen-year-old girl by the name of Collette. She had an unusually long history with Cuba's Department of Intelligence for such a young woman, which raised eyebrows. She was invited by the United States Government to remain in the United States while her husband was incarcerated. She declined; she wanted to return to Cuba. She began calling Cuban officials nonstop, eventually reaching Tony De La Guardia. Given the evidence, Cuba could no longer rely on its default reply to drug smuggling accusations as "Yankee Propaganda." They had to act fast and deflect the accusation from Cuba and the Castro brothers to other individuals.

As a result of all of the surveillance and the debriefing of the Reinaldo & Ruben Ruiz, Operation Greyhound was put into play. This covert operation was a co-op of multiple departments involving; the US Attorney's Office in the Southern District of Florida, United States Customs, DEA, and DIA (Defense Intelligence Agency). The navy, air force, elite seal team, squadron of F-16, AWAC, a destroyer, and submarine were all engaged to participate. This operation was so secret that the United States Department of State was not informed.

The objective was to lure Jose Abrantes to a meeting outside Cuban territory by convicted drug smuggler Gustavo "Papito" Fernandez, a former CIA collaborator who was serving a fifty-year sentence on drug trafficking charges. Fernandez had past contacts in Cuba given the fact that he had smuggled three hundred tons of marijuana through the island. In conversations intercepted during the investigation of the original case against Fernandez, according to special agent Patrick O'Brien of the US Customs in charge of South Florida, one name kept coming up. The name was Jose Abrantes, a Cuban general. In order to lure Abrantes outside of Cuba, the bait had to be something of great interest to Raul and Fidel Castro. The plan was to convince the Castro brothers and Abrantes that Gustavo Fernandez had information about US satellites flying over Cuba and their capabilities. An exchange was proposed through a third party. The exchange was for 2,000 pounds of cocaine for the documents. However, Fernandez insisted that Abrantes himself be present for the exchange. General Abrantes would then be arrested on the high seas. The plan was put into play.

On June 12, 1989, while under the watchful eye of United States Customs personnel, Fernandez was picked up by two individuals in a motor vehicle and disappeared. That same night Division General Arnaldo Ochoa, and Colonel Tony De La Guardia, were arrested in Cuba along with several others. Cuba's Department of Intelligence was all over the operation. The entire operation had been compromised.

Ochoa and De La Guardia received a visit from Fidel in jail. Fidel Castro was floating a deal; For the good of the revolution, he asked them to publicly clear their superiors and take all the blame for the drug trafficking. If they accepted the deal, he promised them leniency. Fidel was banking on their long-standing relationship and history. Unfortunately for Castro, both De La Guardia and Ochoa had become disenchanted with the revolution and, as a result, declined Fidel's offer.

The stage was set. The cast consisted of decorated Cuban officials along with others. The court-martial was aired on Cuban TV. No, it was not a live broadcast. There was a day or two's delay in the broadcast in order for the government to edit out the information they didn't want the Cuban people and the world to see. Though all arrested and put on trial were following orders at the time, they all became aware they became the scapegoats for the Castro brothers. The trial was strictly controlled by the Castro Brothers. The opening was handled by Raul Castro himself.

After the court-martial, Fidel Castro addressed the Council of State of Cuba. In his address which was aired live in Cuba, he said there had never been a judicial process that involved "so much clarity, so much fairness." He recommended the death penalty in lieu of the 15-year maximum penalty for drug trafficking as prescribed by Cuban law for Colonial Tony De La Guardia, General Arnaldo Ochoa, Major Amando Padron Trujillo, and Captain Jorge Martinez Valdez. On July 13, 1989, all four men were executed. The rest of Castro's patsies were given lengthy prison sentences.

Many say the four executed were chosen to be executed as the Castro brothers felt they no longer believed in the revolution and could not be trusted to carry their narrative. Aside from Ochoa's failure to exonerate the Castro brothers, his popularity among the Cuban people sealed his fate. General Arnaldo Ochoa was Cuba's most decorated military officer, the triumphant leader in Angola, and a hero of the revolution. So, like Che, Ochoa's popularity was a threat that had to be neutralized. What better way than to criminalize him. Unfortunately for Fidel, most Cubans and the world saw right through his theater.

The sham of a trial did little to nothing to the narcotics trade in Cuba and the Castro brothers' involvement. It was business as usual. To the world, Fidel saved face with the execution and incarceration of the "so-called traffickers." Fidel declared, "when it comes to narcotics trafficking, Cuba is clean," all the while continuing to develop a sophisticated drug trafficking business. He strengthened his ties to the Colombian guerrillas, Venezuela, and the Mexican cartels.

As for the smugglers that cooperated with United States authorities in operation Greyhound? Reinaldo Ruiz died of a heart attack while in federal custody on December 31, 1990. Ruben Ruiz was convicted of drug trafficking. After cooperating with authorities to indict several Cuban government officials, Johnny Crump began living under an assumed name at an undisclosed location as part of the Federal Witness Protection Program. However, his Cuban associate Rene Rodriguez Diaz, Johnny Crump's co-defendant and his link to Castro, died in late 1989 in Habana of a mysterious illness.

Mario Estevez, the Cuban intelligence officer who implicated Rodriguez Diaz, also had an untimely demise in an American prison shortly thereafter. Among those that were sentenced to prisons terms in Cuba, Captain Miguel Ruiz Poo was sentenced to 30 years in prison. I'm sure he received such a lengthy term due to his performance in the court-martial; he said that Cuba's cocaine smuggling operation had been approved at the highest levels. Shortly after that statement, he appeared faint, a recess was taken, and subsequently, the court session was adjourned for the day. The following day when Poo was returned to court, he was heavily drugged, and he walked his comments back by stating nobody had discussed anything about drugs at the highest levels.

The conditions in Cuba haven't changed; what has changed is their allegiance. After Russia bailed on Cuba, Venezuela and China stepped in. Even with the change in allegiance, Cuba's economy is still in shambles. The old adage "what has happened will invariably happen again when the same circumstances which combine to produce it shall again combine in the same way," comes into play here. The circumstances in Cuba are the same and therefore, Cuba will continue to fund its country and its revolution the only way they know how.

Chapter 19: Sociology, Dad, And Drug Lords

During my college education, I had to take sociology. I had a really interesting teacher; he was a former military man, army. The first discussion in the class was the Korean war. My professor made it very clear the official dates of the United States involvement were 1950-1953, but the United States was present in Korea years prior to the war. A student asked him why. The professor basically told him whenever the United States is involved in any war, they are involved in the area for several years before any actual war breaks out via the CIA and other government entities.

Oh joy, just the class I really wanted to take. The most interesting part of this class was actually watching my fellow students' reactions to this type of news. The word naive doesn't even come close to explaining the student body in this class and its notions of the world at large. My classmates had this ideological idea that democracy survives by singing Kumbaya with other countries. Most were in shock to find out that was not the case. I couldn't imagine how they would have reacted if I opened my mouth and began to discuss what I knew; their heads would have exploded!

There wasn't anything shocking to me in this class; most of it I already knew. I had first-hand knowledge. What I took away from the class was our government, the CIA, involvement in the narcotics trade involving opium, heroin, cocaine, and marijuana. The CIA's role and involvement in various forms; complicity, tolerance, or willful ignorance about the trade. They did not have any direct culpability in the actual trafficking, but it did provide its assets, allies, and drug lords with transport, arms, and political protection. Precisely, the CIA's role in most narcotic trade involved indirect complicity rather than direct culpability. Our government and its agencies operated and continue to operate under the definition of plausible deniability. Then again, so do all of the other countries across this globe.

Of course, I knew from my conversations with my father regarding the United States' presence in any specific region prior to any conflict and or war breaking out. I recall in late 1978, a conversation that occurred between my parents regarding an offer my father had received for a new assignment in Saudi Arabia. He was being sent to the region due to the instability in the area, primarily the radicalization of Iran and the threat it posed to the United States interest in the petroleum trade in the region.

Though only nine years old, I was being recruited by my father to encourage my mother with this new "adventure." He made it sound fun. It didn't matter how many people my father tried to recruit to this effort, there was no way in hell my mother was going to sign off on this new assignment. Since our arrival in Los Angeles, my mother went to work for a middle eastern family as their bookkeeper. She was exposed to the Muslim religion and its ideology toward women. Her employers provided funding to organizations like Hamas, and Yasser Arafat had made several visits to their offices. You would have thought my father would have known anything having to do with the middle east would have been dead on arrival, so why would he even go down that road? He thought…no, he really thought there was an actual possibility of success.

My mother's office was located in Hollywood on the corner of Hollywood Blvd. and Vine St. My brother, father, and I went to pick her up at work in our green Chevy Nova. She entered the car, and they began their idle chitchat of the day. The chitchat would eventually lead to her asking how his day was. He told her he had received an offer and just left that statement hanging out there. My father, the avid fisherman, threw the bait out and was waiting to see if she took it. She took the bait, and he began reeling her in slowly. As he continued down Vine St., my mom looked at him and said, "Are you going to tell me?"

"No, I'm not sure about it yet; once I am, we will talk about it, but nothing to worry about now," he said.

We made it back to our apartment on Rossmore Blvd when she picked up the conversation again. She asked him if it involved Central America. He replied no and told her not to worry about it. I had a front-row seat at this production. The coyer he was about the matter, the more it piqued her interest. It took him a few days before he played his last hand.

Dad told Mom the assignment was in the middle east, and she, along with my brother and I, would live in Saudi Arabia. He would be based out of Saudi Arabia but would be dealing with issues concerning Iran, Libya, and American oil interest in the region. My mother was silent for a few minutes; then she questioned, "American Oil Interest?" He replied, "The American government's interest in the region is the oil." She said, "The United States has plenty of oil reserves here. Why should we care about the oil over there? Why are we making them rich by buying their oil?"

He looked at her at said, "We have elevated that region because they have oil. Yes, we have oil, but we will not use our oil until we have exhausted all of theirs and leave them without any salable natural resource. We won't tap our resources until they are bled dry." He went on to paint a pretty picture; "We would live in the American community, and my brother and I would attend American Schools. It would expose us to new cultures." After that comment, my mother jumped in and stopped him from finishing his picture.

Mom unloaded on Dad. She told him she absolutely would not be moving to any middle eastern country, let alone any Muslim country. She said he could go if he wanted to but disagreed to herself or us, her children, joining him. She looked at him and said she would not wear a niqab, burka, or headscarf. She would not walk behind him and would never allow her daughter to be treated like a second-class citizen. She ended her tirade. "You've lost your fucking mind!" Just like that, the fisherman watched as his line snapped and watched his fish get away.

Weeks after that conversation, the Shah of Iran fled into exile, and less than 24 months after that, the Iranian hostage crisis began. My father was approached about an assignment in that region just weeks before chaos was breaking out and two years before the hostage mess began. I used this memory and what was going on in my sociology class to approach my dad.

I arrived home after class mid-afternoon. He was watching TV, and I brought up the entire Saudi Arabia thing; it brought a smile to his face and a chuckle. He looked at me and said, you remember that? I said yes. I then began to talk to him about my sociology class and some of the things being discussed.

I brought up the Korean War and the Golden Triangle. The definition of the Golden Triangle as represented in class was the area of Southeast Asia; Burma, Laos, and Thailand are the major source of heroin in the world. As I continued, my father abruptly stopped me. He told me there are two definitions of the Golden Triangle. He said the one I gave is one of them, but there is another. During the Korean War, intelligence from the area relied on by Washington was also referred to as "The Golden Triangle."

He looked at me and said, you already know the CIA was in the area before the war. They are always in any area well before any conflict or war. He said that was somewhere around 1949. The war started in 1950. Everyone, The United States and The United Nations, thought this conflict would be resolved quickly, and that would have been the case had China not gotten involved in it. However, China jumped into the fray supporting North Korea. Essentially, this war was between the United States and Communist China.

I looked at him, and before I could get the question out, he stopped me. He told me not to interrupt him. The United States needed information about the Chinese. The company turned to tribal warlords to sneak American assets into China. In return for this service, the United States would equip the warlords with arms. The intelligence flowing from this arrangement to the United States was called the "The Golden Triangle." I waited and didn't interrupt him but asked why the same name why be associated with drug trafficking?

"The tribes have always cultivated opium; it was their cash crop. The choice of their cash crop was not the business of the CIA. The company didn't condone it, but it also didn't stop it. In return for their cooperation and providing information, the CIA turned a blind eye to tribal warlords opium business. Why the same name, I really don't know. This game makes for odd bedfellows, he said, but Korea isn't the only case.

You know about the whole Iran Contra debacle. There it wasn't heroin; it was cocaine. I interjected and said yes, but in that instance, CIA assets were running drugs." He looked at me and said, "In most instances, most successful CIA assets became drug traffickers. Very successful traffickers at that. He saw the look on my face, and he said hold on a minute – not me but quite a few that you have known have."

I said, "Why aren't they in jail?"

He looked at me and said, "Really…you really don't know why or you want me to confirm what you already suspect?" I said, "I had my suspicions, but I've learned not to assume anything in this family." He laughed and said, "Those assets that were in the game for a lengthy period of time dealing with very powerful politicians. Just as you saw in the Contra hearings, political theater is the name of the game. If any politician is caught with knowledge of and or linked to non-congressional authorized operations, their political life is over, and they could face charges; Political blackmail. The assets know the rules of the game; keep it below the radar the government will turn a blind eye. In many instances, The company ran interference in some cases by not sharing or allowing the DEA to do its job.

This policy didn't just apply to assets turned drug traffickers but also to allies. Manuel Noriega amassed his fortune from the drug trade. The United States was fully aware of it but did nothing for decades because he was an ally. Noriega wasn't a communist; he was assisting in the United States in Nicaragua against the Sandinistas. This has been going on since the times of the OSS (Office of Strategic Services) and World War II."

There have been innuendos, accusations, and assertions regarding the CIA for that fact, the United States government has had some interactions with the drug trade. Let's start with the CIA's predecessor, the office of strategic services. It was formed in 1942 during World War II; its primary purpose was to collect and analyze strategic information and to conduct special operations not assigned to other agencies. Odd bedfellows are an understatement when it comes to World War II.

The OSS, along with other United States agencies, cultivated relations with the leaders of the Italian Mafia, recruiting heavily from the New York and Chicago families, whose members included Charles 'Lucky' Luciano, Meyer Lansky, Joe Adonis, and Frank Costello. They helped these agencies keep in touch with Sicilian Mafia leaders exiled by Italian dictator Benito Mussolini. "Lucky" Luciano assisted in the control of our East Coast ports. These relations also provided intelligence on Sicily prior to the allied invasions and helped in suppressing the Italian Communist Party. "Lucky" would receive a pardon for his wartime efforts and be deported to Italy, where he would continue his involvement in the heroin trade.

Continuing the U.S. intelligence community's anti-communist drive, the OSS worked with the Corsican gang in France to maintain control of the Old Port of Marseilles from the hands of the French Communist Party. In return, a blind eye was given to them and their heroin trade. Luciano and the Corsicans came together and would dominate the global heroin trade for two and half decades. This joint venture would come to be known as the French Connection and would come to an end in the early 1970s.

In 1945, the OSS was dissolved, and the CIA emerged. In 1950 The United States was involved in the Korean war.

Just as my father had too told me, the CIA struck a deal with local Asian tribal warlords to smuggle assets into and out of China, and in return, they were allowed to continue their heroin trade unhampered by the United States. There have been rumors of CIA front company, Air America, providing air services to the local warlords for the trafficking of heroin to the United States as part of their arrangement.

Then we come to Nicaragua, the fight for central America. What started as anti-communist and anti-Castro operations turned into a game of communism, guns, drugs, and hostages. It was a war, but it was an undeclared war waged to keep communism and socialism out of the United States' backyard. Here is where the emergence of ex-CIA assets became traffickers. They would be among the most successful traffickers due to their experience and having plenty of information on politicians and officials. Information, if released, would ruin the politicians and officials and possibly lead to incarceration.

After Nicaragua came Panama, Manuel Noriega was a one-time American ally but also neck-deep in the drug trade. Drugs were being funneled through Panama, money laundered through Panamanian banks, and then there was the ultimate betrayal in 1986, Noriega was selling information on the United States to the Cuban Government. The selling of intelligence to enemies of the United States was the straw that broke the camel's back. The United States was looking for any excuse to enter Panama. Noriega's forces began harassing U.S. troops and civilians in Panama. The death of First Lieutenant Robert Paz of the United States Marine Corps by Panamanian troops gave the United States the excuse they were looking for to invade Panama. His death, along with the harassment of American Citizens, was the primary excuse and the justification given to the American population to invade Panama and remove Noriega. Truth be told, the invasion was already in the works when the death of the soldier occurred. Noriega was removed and brought to the United States to stand trial.

Then there is Columbia, Venezuela, Mexico, Honduras, Afghanistan, and the list goes on. The bottom line, all intelligence communities operate within these realms. All countries, ours included, have strange bedfellows when it suits their needs. The ends justify the means, and all those in the way are removed. Those in good graces today will eventually be on the outs. Unfortunately for them, that means exile, prosecution, incarceration, death, or all of the above.

Chapter 20: Opie And Mayberry

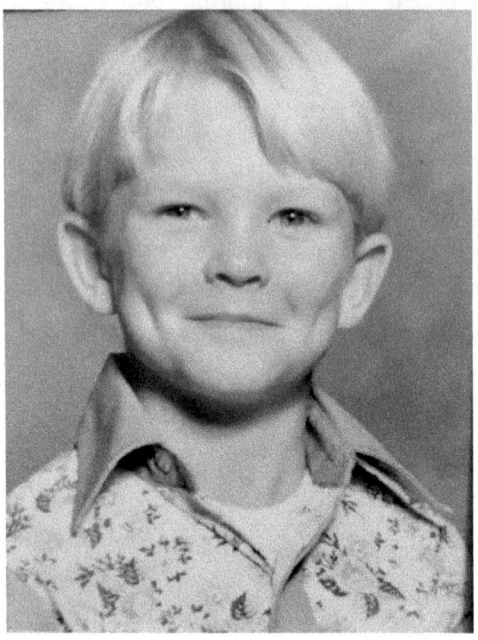

By the time I was twenty years old, I was living in Fresno, California, with my parents and siblings – a normal, quiet life. When my parents moved to Fresno originally, I opted to move to Miami and live with my grandparents. After eighteen months of Miami life, I was ready to return to life as a student. I moved to Fresno in April 1987.

Talk about a normal life! An old adage came to my mind again: "Be careful what you wish for." A normal life!? Wow, what a concept! Fresno was so far from any kind of life I had ever experienced. It definitely took getting used to.

I enrolled in the local community college. In the fall semester of 1988, I was set up on a blind date by a classmate.

He was everything I would not date, and I was everything he would not date. Within days of meeting, we were inseparable.

This guy was an open book. Born and raised in the same small town just North of Fresno. He was the son of a contractor and had three other older siblings. He was simple. I, on the other hand, was complicated. All he knew was my family was Cuban, my father worked for a major raisin company, my mother owned a small grocery store in his hometown, and I had two younger siblings. He could introduce me to friends he had gone to school with since kindergarten, a fat chance of that happening with me.

He told me early on he always envisioned marrying a hometown girl whose family he'd known all his life. He would know everything about her. Boy, did he hook up with the wrong girl! He had no idea the ride he was in for. Inevitably, the questions began.

"Why did y'all move so much? Were you an army brat?" When I told him no, I was a government brat, he asked what part of the government. I tried to deflect that question for as long as I could, but finally, I had to answer. I told him and waited. He would later tell me he thought I was nuts; he said my answer sounded like the kids in grade school:

"Oh yeah, well …my dad can beat your dad up, well. Well, oh yeah. Well, my dad is Superman and your dad Lex Luthor and my dad always beats your dad."

He did not share that with me for about four weeks after I told him. Even though my dad made comments during that time that referred to his association with the company, it was not until I gave him documents to review that it finally hit home with him. This was no bullshit.

It happened on a trip to Los Angeles to attend the famous rival football classic between UCLA and USC. My father had instructed me to retrieve some documents a very close family friend had. My father told me I should share the documents. I thought for a moment about what my dad told me to do, and it made sense. Either this guy was going to run for the hills and think I'm a nut, or he will stand firm and think we are all nuts. I had nothing to lose.

I collected the documents as instructed, and on our way back home, we stopped at a fast-food restaurant at the base of the grapevine to eat. I gave him the manila envelope and told him to open it and begin reading. He had been reading for a few minutes when he stopped to look at me and said, "You're serious!" He told me he had believed I was nuts, and was happy I wasn't, but at the same time, he could not believe what he was reading.

The documents he was reading were on the JFK assassination. He read about the triangular shots, the players involved in his death, and basically, the setup of an American President. He now understood my realm of reality. In an instant, I took Opie out of Mayberry.

He was born and raised in Small Town, USA. He knew who he was, he knew what he was going to be, and he knew what he wanted out of life. He knew. Until I walked into his life, he was certain he knew all he needed or wanted to know, and in that instant, it all changed. He was staring at government documentation that directly contradicted what his history book had taught him. Now the questions really came at me.

After a while, he directed his questions to my dad, and my dad willingly answered them. Dad seemed to know this was the man who was going to walk through life with me, and it was important to my dad that he knew everything. …well, as much of everything as possible. Finally, someone I could share all of it with, someone to who I could tell my fears to and they would understand the root of those fears. For a long time, I thought he was eventually going to run for the hills, but he stuck it out. We married in 1990, and yes, I moved to Small Town, USA. For the first time in my 21 years, I was living a normal life. I was finally like the girl next door. I was lucky I did not have to be the one to tell my in-laws about my dad. My husband covered that one. Boy, that must have been one hell of a conversation:

"Mom and dad, you know the girl I've been seeing? Well, you see, her family is a little bit different, not because they are Cuban, but her dad sort of worked for the government. He blew up a few things, shot up and burned a Spanish cargo vessel, and extracted diplomats. You know, just like the neighbors down the street."

It was hard enough to muster the nerve to tell him, but to tell his parents? I would have preferred to face a firing a squad first. Truth be told, they were, and have been great about all of it. I am finally the girl next door…and Opie? Well, let's just say he is no longer in Mayberry.

Chapter 21: 1990's
(Resegregation, slavery, unraveling of the United States' constitution, political correctness, China, and social media)

As a product of my upbringing, the United States' education system, political system, and the American populous shaped how I see and read the world. I was born 14 years after the Brown v. Board of Education decision, which began the desegregation of this country. As a child through my teens, I was taught discrimination based on ethnicity, color, sex, and religion had no place in this country, and it was against the law.

The desegregation and the unification of the populous began in 1954 as a result of that decision, along with the civil rights movement. It was an era of activism for equal rights and treatment of colored Americans in the United States. Americans from all walks of life, ethnicity, color, sex, and religion rallied for social, legal, political, and cultural changes to ban discrimination and end segregation. Peaceful civil rights leaders like Martin Luther King spoke of unity and equality for all. He came along before me and died before me as well.

As I grew up, I heard and watched how our country "categorized" its populous. Up until 1986, most if not all paperwork had basic categories; male, female, black, white,

Latin, American Indian, and others. Regardless of any of those labels, all in the populous were Americans. Don't get me wrong, we all identify within our ethnicity/culture, but we were all Americans. We enjoyed experiencing and learning about other cultures as Americans. As desegregation was in full swing and minorities (as labeled by others, not me) made strides, leaving discrimination on the downward trend, I saw and understood why my father chose to do what he did. The life and opportunities afforded to all Americans was available to all.

In the 1990's, I saw that forward trend come to a screeching halt. Government documents, including school documents, began segregating the populous again as hyphenated Americans; African-American, Mexican-American, Asian-American, German-Americans, Irish-Americans, etc. After almost 40 years, Brown v. Board of education, and we have allowed ourselves to be segregated AGAIN! I sat down with my dad and discussed this.

He saw I was absolutely shocked that Americans have allowed themselves to be segregated. He looked at me and said, "United we stand, divided we fall." I glanced back at him and said, "Abraham Lincoln? What does Abraham Lincoln have to do with this discussion?" He said the same thing that Benjamin Franklin did: "They, along with our government, specifically this administration, know all too well the power of the people when united. There is a lot of truth in the phrase; divide and conquer."

He continued, "Segregating by classification, they are dividing the people. You see," he said, "although we have a constitution and laws, they don't take into consideration the human condition. Conceit, being full of oneself is how it was sold under the guise of "Political Correctness." Americans would never knowingly allow themselves to be segregated again, but by distinguishing oneself as a hyphenated American, you are part of a special group. This administration isn't resegregating anyone; they are simply making them feel special—what a great marketing plan."

"As we are sorted into our little boxes, they whisper to each category what it wants to hear in order to gain popularity and retain its positions—this puts one category against another. By keeping the populous separated, this administration is securing itself for another term in office and setting the foundation for the theft of life, liberty, and the pursuit of happiness, robbing all Americans of their constitutional rights.

"This isn't the first time it has happened in history. Look through history, and you will find many examples. I only have to look back at Cuba, and all the signs are there."

He put his hands up and did air quotes uttering the term "Political Correctness." He said, "Political correctness violates one's freedom of speech. When you can no longer speak freely, you cease being a free country; you become an enslaved country. When polls become more important than following the basic principles this country was founded on, we are a step closer to becoming another Cuba. In order for "Political Correctness" to work, you have to compartmentalize/resegregate the populous and create friction within the divided group. A divided population will not recognize what is being done. Keeping them distracted keeps them from seeing what is really going on. By the time they realize it, if they ever do, the freedoms afforded to all will be whittled away. This administration is chipping away at the constitution.

"When the government starts banning speech and what books you can read, you need to be very afraid. When there is no longer a free press but a controlled press delivering selective narrative and suppressing the flow of information, that's a problem, but none of this will ring any alarm bells with the populous because they are being distracted by "Political Correctness.""

"I get it," I told him. "I don't like what I am seeing and hearing. What's the distraction? Is it the Middle East?" He said, "No, it's China." I looked at him and said, "China?"

He said, "Yes, China. While most of America are asleep at the wheel, China is on the move, and they are very dangerous. The Soviet Union has nothing on the Chinese, and America better wake up before it's too late. This administration has been bought and paid for by China. These new trade agreements given to the Chinese will open up their economy and markets."

"Isn't an open economy a good thing for China?" I asked. He looked at me and said, "China is a communist country. Everything is owned by the government. Doing business with Chinese companies is doing business with the Chinese government. China is among the most populated countries in the world, an untapped consumer group." For a moment, I thought, what the hell do consumers have to do with this, and before I could ask it, he continued. "China, for its size, is an underdeveloped country in many ways. It is lagging behind in technology and military capabilities. These trade agreements allow for the partnering of American companies, American technology to be shared with Chinese companies—" I interrupted him and said, "We are going to give them our technology?" He said, "Yes. This administration has sold our technology and did it right in front of the American public under the guise of economic assistance. Some would say a humanitarian effort and to question any of it would be "Politically Incorrect.""

"I don't understand why isn't the pentagon and the CIA screaming about this?" I asked. He said, they are, but this administration has such disdain for them they have drowned them out. The foundation they are laying will have long-term consequences for this country and its citizens. Pay close attention when this president leaves office; he will be a very wealthy man. The money he is paid for being president won't come close to affording the lifestyle he will have. This president is as corrupt, if not more so than Batista was. He is not there to serve this country; he is there to serve himself and feed his greed – he is no different than Castro.

"He picked up a few ceramic pieces he had collected over the years and flipped them over, and asked me to read what was stamped on the bottom. I read them; one said 'made in Taiwan,' another 'made in Japan.' He said, "You watch everything now will be made in China. People in this country will lose their manufacturing jobs with this trade deal. This country was a powerhouse of manufacturing and industry; that's how we won World War II. Now everything is made elsewhere, and this country is turning into a country of paper pushers and consumers. When a country stops producing necessary and vital products, it ceases being self-sufficient and must rely on others, and that is a very dangerous position to be in.""

On the ride home after dinner, I couldn't help but think about my discussion with him. He was proud I had caught onto and was questioning the segregation and the "political correctness" issues, but I was disappointed in myself for not catching the whole China equation. He was right; the human condition wasn't being taken into account. The selling out of America, its people, and its future to line one's pocket was being ignored or, better said, concealed by "political correctness."

I was in my early twenties when the term "political correctness" was on various news channels and newspapers. At the time, I thought the term was coined then, but now I know better. I bet most Americans have no idea where that term originated from. It also makes me question if they did know if it would even matter?

"Political correctness" first appeared in Marxist-Leninist vocabulary following the Russian Revolution of 1917. It encompassed the policies and principles of the Communist Party. It was used to adhere to the party line. Here in the United States in the late 1970s and into the 1980s, it was used by liberal politicians to refer to the extremism of some left-wing agenda, particularly regarding an emphasis on rhetoric over the content.

Then there was the 1990's the Clinton's Administrations use of the term and the media's weaponization of the term. Then and now, "political correctness" is the cause of censorship and the curtailment of freedom of speech in this country. From 1993 to date, I watched as the media ceased being journalists and morphed into opinionated political hacks. They were skewing the truth and placing a political spin to fit their narrative and shape their outcome. Anyone who dare challenge them, out flies the term "political correctness" to promote the notion of offensive language where none exists. In doing this, they discredit and destroy the individual who challenged them and diminish the freedoms provided in our constitution.

I have witnessed the evolution of this country's resegregation. Not just by ethnicity, but sex, sexual orientation, religion, etc. Any label is used to further the resegregation of this country. I thought for a brief moment on September 11, 2001, that there was hope. On that day, when this country was attacked, everyone in the country stood up, and for the first time in eight years, I heard, "American," not a hyphenated American but just American. All of the subcategories went away. A glimmer of light and hope was extinguished just as quickly as it began.

So, why has our government, a government for the people and by the people, embraced governmental ethnic-based discrimination? The consequences of "political correctness" and resegregation is the concept that people should be judged by the color of their skin, gender, sexual orientation not equally or as individuals. This has been done to promote a socialist agenda. What better way than to say,

"You see, you are being treated differently based on whatever reason, and that's discrimination. However, we can solve it by we the government stepping in and taking care of you, and your every need equally. Everyone will be treated and paid the same. You no longer work for yourselves, your dreams, your goals. You work for everyone's goals. You work for the government and its goals."

Slavery in its basic form typically involves the enslaved person being made to perform some form of work while also having their location dictated by the enslaver. Their wellbeing is in the hands of their slave master, not their own. The slave is not allowed free speech, free movement/travel, free to assemble, etc. Their compensation is provided by their slave master.

Any form of socialism is SLAVERY. Communism is SLAVERY. Welfare is SLAVERY. Most folks don't realize socialism and communism believe that economic revolution will ultimately solve all societal injustices, such as ethnic inequalities. From an economic standpoint, Marx's theory that ethnic differences could be solved if the entire population was not compartmentalized and labeled but all were treated the same economically has been proven a failure. Further, it is a form of slavery.

You need only look 90 miles to the south to see how well that worked out. Everyone on the Island of Cuba, with the exception of the Castro's and a select few politicians, are treated the same economically: SQUALOR. However, the ethnic divide has not been eradicated aside from the squalor that unites all these groups is their enslavement.

The one thing my father did not live to see was the rise of social media – a platform that was originally designed for folks to stay in touch with one another soon turned into a political weapon. Unfortunately, these platforms tout a free space for expression. They are not. They are no different than any other corporation. Corporations are out there for a profit and, as such, will capitulate to the current popular narrative and squash all other forms of speech. In doing so, they sacrifice the basic human rights of all for their profit, the profit of their shareholders, and for their political agenda advancement. They have a monopoly, not unlike the large oil corporations of the early 1900s, which were ultimately broken up by the Sherman Antitrust Act and they should face the same.

California's attempt to resegregate and legalize discrimination failed. In November 2020, California's populous struck down Proposition 16, a decision-making policy that considers race, sex, color, ethnicity, or national origin to supposedly address diversity. Diversity is being used to re-introduce and legalize discrimination based on all of the categories that we as a populous so despise and worked for decades to eradicate. It is no coincidence the "Woke" movement began right about the same time. California voters may have balked at legalized discrimination, but corporations are seemingly happy to embrace and inject ethnic categories, resegregation, and discrimination into their business models to follow the "Woke" movement model.

While we as American's have been so distracted by categorizing ourselves and discriminating against ourselves with our government leading the way, one has to wonder if this is not yet another distraction. What could we be distracted from? China!

In my travels throughout Central and South America, along with the Caribbean from the end of the Clinton Administration to date, I have seen China's presence in every country in the region. China has enslaved several countries by providing funding for the future sale of the natural resources as well as controlling trade routes; Venezuela – crude oil, Brazil – iron ore, Brazil – crude oil, Trinidad/Tobago, Liquefied Natural Gas, and Panama China operates the ports at each end of the canal; Balboa and Cristobal. These are just a few examples. Recently all Americans, as well as the rest of the world, realized China owns most of the ingredients/natural resources for medications. China provides the United States with most of its medications.

Fun fact; According to the U.S. Commerce Department, Chinese pharmaceutical firms provide 97% of antibiotics and more than 90% of Vitamin C to the United States. In 2018, 95% of ibuprofen, 91% of hydrocortisone, 70% of acetaminophen, and 40-45% of heparin imported to the United States came from China.

Most over-the-counter and generic drugs sold in the United States are made in China, including antidepressants, HIV/AIDS medications, birth control pills, chemotherapy treatments, and medicines for Alzheimer's disease, diabetes, epilepsy, and Parkinson's disease. Clinton's policies have put the United States medical independence at risk along with the health of each and every American, not to mention the exportation of industry and manufacturing.

Until COVID-19 (Wuhan Virus) struck the world, most Americans were completely unaware of how much of the world market China controls. Most Americans are blinded by "diversity" and have allowed themselves to be resegregated, which will lead to the enslavement of the entire population. Most American's no longer read a text in its entirety, only the talking points presented by the media, social media, and politicians. The majority of Americans identify themselves as hyphenated Americans. Until

Americans refer to themselves as Americans, come together as Americans, and stand up as Americans, the United States will be divided and shall be conquered.

Epilogue

No, we were not the typical American Family. We are Americans to the purest form of the word. All of the losses suffered by my family at the hands of Castro and his regime led them to fight for the preservation of the American Constitution. Though this book only discusses one of them, there were more who went out and fought to preserve the American Constitution and the freedoms it provides. I might look like the typical American girl next door, but I am not. I know there are so many children out there like me whose fathers, mothers, or other family members run below the radar working for the government, commonly referred to as "assets."

Those assets put their lives on the line so we, the American public, may enjoy the freedoms afforded us in the constitution. Their families must deal with their absence, the danger their lives bring, and the reality they may never return just so we can live and be safe. These families look just like your neighbors. In fact, they are. Yes, I am all grown up and understand the reality of our world. Unfortunately, my father did not live to see the day Fidel Castro died, but it is also fortunate that he did not live to see what Cuba is today.

As Russia emerged from communism, Cuba lost its biggest benefactor, it's master. As communism went by the wayside, the romance of socialism once again was emerging on the island. Without Russia's money, Cuba was in a very precarious state. Then entered Venezuela and Hugo Chavez. Yes, Fidel sought and obtained support in Venezuela, but it too faded. Upon his death, his brother Raul took the reins of the country.

For the purpose of the world stage, Raul Castro retired in 2018, and Miguel Mario Diaz-Canel Bermudez became the president. In 2019, I, along with my family, traveled to Cuba; for everyone but my mother, it was the first visit to Cuba. For her, it was returning after 60 years. I know it is odd to say, but there was a familiarity to Habana although I had never been there. I recognized multiple neighborhoods and buildings. I, along with my siblings and other family members, learned to love a country we had never been to but through photos.

The best way to describe Cuba is dilapidated elegance. You can still see what Cuba once was. Her beauty, her wealth, and what is left of it. Though her buildings and streets are crumbling, her people are the gems she stills holds. My group had the pleasure of traveling with local guides. I, as did they, learned the truth of current-day Cuba.

I learned there is still a two-class system: the Castro regime – "The Haves," and the rest of the population – "The Have Nots." Our tour guide was a wealth of information. As usual, I began to ask questions. I asked him if he had always been a tour guide? He said No, by education, he is an engineer. As an engineer, he made the U.S. equivalent $30.00 a month. His housing is provided – if you can call it housing, and he had food rations. This is supposed to sustain his wife and children. So, when Cuba allowed some free enterprise, he took a job as a tour guide. This paid him the U.S. equivalent of $400.00 a month, not including tips.

Most Americans are of the notion that Cuba's main source of revenue is its export of sugar, tobacco, and tobacco-related products. My husband was no different. He asked me to ask the tour guide about what was their biggest export. His response shocked us all. He replied, "Its people." As usual, I could not let this go by without delving further into his comment. I asked, "What do you mean 'it's people'?"

He looked at me. "Cuba's sugar and tobacco crop were once king, but that faded long ago. So, the Cuban government had to harvest a new crop, its people. It takes its children and educates them. It sorts them based on the ability for higher education. Of course, this education is free," he said with a smirk. "You and I and everyone in this world knows nothing is free. Once the education is complete, these children are doctors, engineers, biologists, teachers, mechanics, etc. The government then contracts with other countries for these trades, and they are sent to these countries to work. He said his wife had just come back from a year in Peru; she was a psychiatrist. Peru paid Cuba the U.S. equivalent of $350,000.00 for her services, and Cuba, in return, paid her monthly salary the equivalent of $40.00 U.S. dollars. Her housing and food were provided for when she was there. In short, the Cuban people are no more than slave labor."

Our group asked our tour guides if they could take us to the closest local beach. I had always heard Cuba's beaches were absolutely stunning. Santa Maria del Mar was a short ride from Habana. As we walked out onto the beach, we observed that the water was stunning, but the beach was filthy. There was trash, mainly bottles, everywhere, and the locals of Cuba that were there were still throwing empty bottles of beer and soda cans in the sand. I was shocked.

I turned to my tour guide as we walked back to the car, and asked why the beach was so filthy if tourism was such a huge part of the Cuban economy. He looked and me and said, "Ay Mi Amor (oh my love). This beach is for the locals; this is not a tourist beach." In the same breath, he said, "The tourist beaches are cleaned and combed daily. For a long time, we were not allowed at the tourist beach. We can go now, but we have to pay to get in".

As our group left the beach, I saw a small local store with some tables came up on the right-hand side and asked if we could stop for lunch there. He said, "No, that's not for you; that is for the locals. You'll be lucky if it has sodas, but I'll take you somewhere all of our clients go to and absolutely love. He made a phone call and made our reservation. As we entered Habana, I asked him if the food was good where we were going. He said, "All of our clients love it." I looked at him and said, "No, I am asking you if the food is good there?" He said, "I've never eaten there."

Once again, I had to push the envelope. "What do you mean you have never eaten there? He said, "I can't afford to eat there. Don't get me wrong, we have our restaurants that serve the same dishes, but the food grade is different for us than for the tourists." At that moment, I wished I had never asked the question. We arrived for lunch and asked him to join us, but he declined.

After lunch, our guide realized I and the rest of us were a bit uncomfortable. He said, "Look, you must know as does the rest of Cuban populous that Castro's revolution is a failure. We went from a free two-class system to an enslaved single-class system. What I say to you here in this car is the same thing I say in my house, but do not dare say it in public. It would land me in jail.". I looked at him and asked, "Then why stay?" He said, "If we all leave, there would be no one to push for change. Make no mistake; there is a revolution going on here. No, it won't be a revolution with guns but with information. The internet has come, and the government realizes their propaganda doesn't work. Change is slow. We went from communism to socialism. Both systems are terrible and enslave the populous. Change is slow, but it is change."

As we closed our day and conversations, I asked about the-then president and if, upon Raul Castro's death, there will be free democratic elections in Cuba. He laughed and said, "Raul hasn't stepped down. All of that was for the world community; they found him too old and out of touch to truly be part of the world community. In an effort to show the world that Cuba was truly opening up, abandoning communism, and embracing a form of socialism, he hand-picked Miguel Mario Diaz-Canel Bermudez. The Castro family will never give up Cuba – its tyrannical rule. When Raul dies, there will be elections, of course, but it will be Raul's son-in-law, the general, who will take over, if not his son. The elections will be a show for the world, but we Cubans already know who is coming next."

Returning to the port, we could not help but notice all the brand-new Chinese construction equipment and construction infrastructure supplies. Of course, I couldn't keep my mouth shut. As I pointed, he nodded his head yes. "Los Chinos – that is who Cuba is in bed with now. They give us everything. Now, as we enter another "special time," the

Castro government will rely on the Chinese more and more." I gave him a look. He said, "Remember I told you our biggest export is our people. Well, we exported a lot of military people to help the Venezuelan president retain control of his country. Your country is not so happy about that, and to be honest, most Cubans aren't either. Your country has banned tourism because we are interfering in Venezuela. To us, the people, this means less money for us and less food. We are already only getting running water three days a week; the rest of the time, our water comes from rainwater storage tanks on the roof. Water is currently rationed out and sparsely supplied. We shall be asked to give up more for the so called greater good of our socialist government."

As my trip to Cuba came to a close, I found myself looking at an island with love and a sense of deep, profound sadness for those still living there. The Castro experiment was an epic fail. It all began with the romanticized vision of socialism, and then there was the reality of it, enslavement. Castro promised change from a two-class system and gave them a single-class system, poverty. There is one thing Castro and the Castro government got right, and that is their people are truly their biggest asset/crop.

Though I understood why my father and other family members did what they did and fought for, after seeing and experiencing Cuba, it became much clearer to me. What they did and others continue to do today, why they fought and continue to fight, is to ensure the United States never becomes another Cuba – that we remain free and not enslaved by the romantic notions of a Utopia of socialism or communism.

My father once told me, "I have been all over the world and experienced other governments though ours is not perfect, it is the best the world has to offer." I agree with that statement.

CPSIA information can be obtained
at www.ICGtesting.com
Printed in the USA
LVHW021135260422
717217LV00015B/773